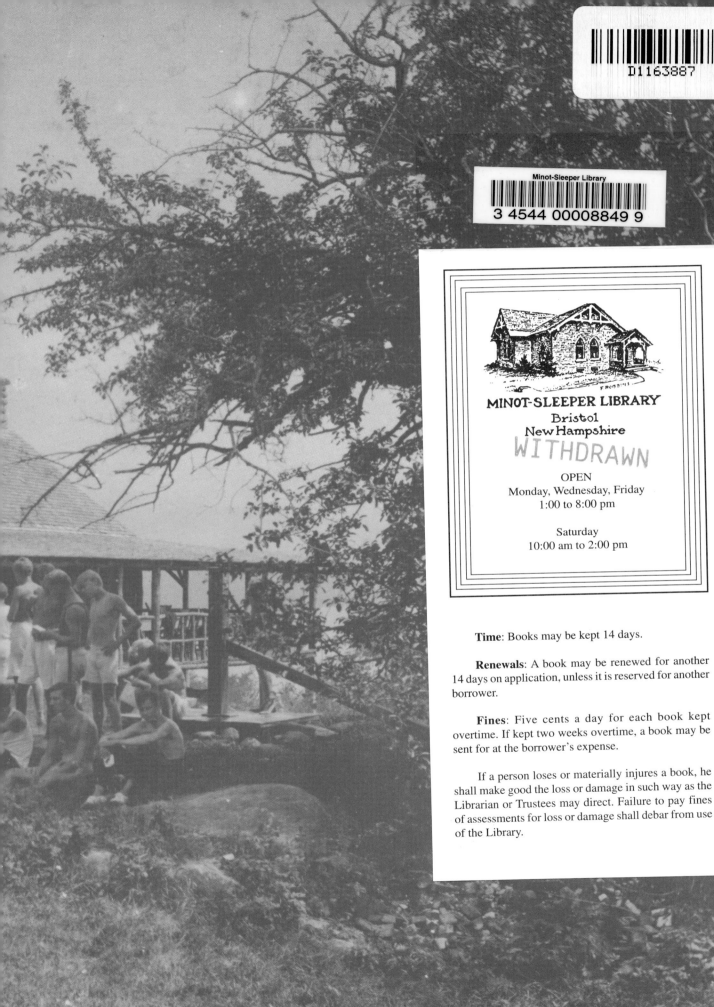

MINOT-SLEEPER LIBRARY
Bristol
New Hampshire
WITHDRAWN

OPEN
Monday, Wednesday, Friday
1:00 to 8:00 pm

Saturday
10:00 am to 2:00 pm

Time: Books may be kept 14 days.

Renewals: A book may be renewed for another 14 days on application, unless it is reserved for another borrower.

Fines: Five cents a day for each book kept overtime. If kept two weeks overtime, a book may be sent for at the borrower's expense.

If a person loses or materially injures a book, he shall make good the loss or damage in such way as the Librarian or Trustees may direct. Failure to pay fines of assessments for loss or damage shall debar from use of the Library.

Camp Tecumseh

1903-1993
Camp Tecumseh

Fred G. Clark

PHOENIX PUBLISHING

West Kennebunk, Maine

Library of Congress Cataloging-in-Publication Data

Clark, Fred G.
  Camp Tecumseh, 1903-1993 / by Fred G. Clark.
  p. cm.
  Includes index.
  ISBN 0-914659-70-7 : $30.00
  1. Camp Tecumseh (N.H.) --History. I. Title.
GV194.N42C373 1994
796.54'2--dc20   94-8224
                                                                        CIP

Copyright 1994 by Camp Tecumseh

Printed in the United States of America

————

This book

is dedicated to the memory of Alexander Grant,

a founder of Camp Tecumseh whose forty-three years

of inspirational leadership won the respect and admiration

of hundreds of campers, staff, and friends. His unselfish last wishes

establishing Tecumseh as a nonprofit perpetual trust

assured continued fulfillment of the mission

and traditions he had initiated.

————

Contents

Introduction

A FEW YEARS AGO as the Trustees of Camp Tecumseh contemplated the approach of the 90th anniversary of its founding, they conceived the idea that the celebration of that event should include publishing a book detailing its history as well as describing through photographs and narrative its uniqueness.

All the Trustees agreed that only someone who had been a camper could convey adequately the mystique of the Tecumseh experience, and that some professional writing experience would also be desirable. Unfortunately, a long look at our alumni list failed to come up with anyone who met these two requirements and appeared able as well as willing to write the book.

During the course of the next few months, however, one name surfaced from the group who, the trustees felt, would be qualified to do the job. He was an alumnus, with his home in Moultonborough, and had done extensive volunteer work organizing and cataloging the massive amount of camp memorabilia which had collected over the years.

The name that surfaced was mine, admittedly an amateur writer, but one who feels that Tecumseh has done more to influence his life than any other single organization. The work, therefore, has been a labor of love and I present this book to you, with the hope that you too will recall old friends and good times from the past, and share the thrill I experienced from rediscovering what Tecumseh really meant to me.

A great many people have contributed ideas, stories, and other material to the making of this book, and it is not possible to thank all of them adequately. Nevertheless, special mention must be made of the many photographs of the early years which come from the albums of co-founder George Orton, and later Charles Wharton, Ed Dawes, Lew Tabor, and Dr. Fred James. During George Munger's directorship, Clint Roth began the task of organizing the voluminous pictures and memorabilia which had accumulated and which Richard Roe later housed in the farmhouse Archive Room. Additional research was done through the medium of twenty-three typed interviews with alumni; and Alexander Grant's daughter, Phyllis Dampman, graciously provided many individual insights into her father's early days, as did Mary Kay Johnson Hargens about her father, Ralph, and uncle, Walter Johnson. The editorial and graphic arts skills of A.A. Paradis and A.L. Morris respectively, of Phoenix Publishing, were essential to the text and design of the book, and Ed Stanley provided guidance and counsel as Chairman of the Book Committee of the Trustees.

Finally, I want to thank my wife Jo for her patience and understanding in putting up with three years of a home cluttered with boxes of memorabilia, and for her unflagging encouragement to see this task completed.

Fred G. Clark

Moultonborough, New Hampshire
November 1, 1993

Camp Tecumseh

1

The Heritage

Before 1903

IN A CURIOUS SORT of way it was the International Championships organized by France as part of the 1900 Exposition at Paris that brought three athletes together who would eventually be the founders of Camp Tecumseh. Actually it was Mike Murphy, track trainer of the University of Pennsylvania, a name Alex Grant often mentioned with fondness and respect, who was responsible for choosing his three outstanding track and field men to participate, namely: Alex Grant, Josiah McCracken, and George Orton.

Michael Charles Murphy grew up in Worcester and Hopkinton, Massachusetts, and became known for his boxing and sprinting abilities. In 1886, Yale University hired him as a coach and trainer for track athletes and he was the first in *any American college* to be given full authority as an athletic director. In his first year at Yale the team won the intercollegiate track and field championship. In 1897 he moved to the University of Pennsylvania and within a year Penn duplicated that performance.

For the last ten years of his life he suffered from tuberculosis (incurable in those years) but with indomitable courage he continued to work with great results to the last. In Penn's final meet against Cornell it was a narrow finish but Penn won. "The team went to Mike's deathbed telling him of the winning of his last intercollegiate contest. Mike died three days later, recognized as the greatest athletic trainer of all time." (*Daily Pennsylvanian*, April 21, 1939)

The 1900 Olympics

It is fitting that we start Camp Tecumseh's history with this tribute to Mike Murphy because of the role he inadvertently played in the camp's history. As mentioned above, the event dates back to the turn of the century when fifty-five athletes from various American universitites (including thirteen from Penn) arrived in Paris.

A substantial number of these athletes on the American team were Christians who took Sunday as a day of rest seriously, and both McCracken and Grant felt strongly on this issue. Athletes from Princeton, Penn, and Syracuse refused to compete on Sunday so the French gave in and agreed to open the games on Saturday, July 14 (a poor day for audience attendance because it was Bastille Day with many competing parades and events) and to let those who had religious convictions against participating on their Sabbath compete on Monday.

However, this was not honored and Sunday events were held. McCracken and Grant were crushed but stuck to their beliefs and did not compromise. George Orton ran anyway and won the 2500 meter steeplechase, and Kraenzlein (later a counselor at Tecumseh) won the broad jump.

On Monday McCracken took a gold in the tug of war, a silver in the shot-put, and a bronze in the hammer throw. The fact that these were Olympic games was only revealed at the end when the medals were awarded. Coach Murphy's team of thirteen men, including his own three star performers, brought in nine gold, seven silver, and four fourth places in a sweep of the 1900 Olympics that some referred to as a "Chariots of Fire" performance in collegiate athletics.

McCracken, Orton, and Grant had become close friends since Murphy had recruited these outstanding track and field men from Kansas and Ontario. Under his direction they became even greater athletes and participated as part of the winning team at the 1899 Intercollegiate championship meet at the University of Pennsylvania. They also worked together as counselors at Camp Idlewild on Cow Island, in Lake Winnipesaukee, and thus the stage was set for the formation of Camp Tecumseh. Because each of these men influenced the development and growth of the camp, it would be interesting to review their individual backgrounds briefly.

Tecumseh's Three Founders

Josiah Calvin McCracken – Kansas Farm Boy

Born in Tennessee on March 30, 1874, he spent little time there since his father, Isaac Lawrence McCracken, and his mother, Ella Watson Stewart, soon moved to a farm in Kansas. Farm work develops strong men, and Josiah was tall and muscular. At Cooper College in Sterling, Kansas, he was on the football team for each of his four years and captain in 1895 when he graduated. In track he kept the 100-yard record most of the time and led in hurdles, but his real skill was in the 16-pound hammer throw where he set the intercollegiate record of 92 feet 8 inches in the State of Kansas. He came in second in the 16-pound shot-put.

Camp Tecumseh

Then Mike Murphy found him and he came to the University of Pennsylvania as a sophomore in the Wharton School in 1896. His parents had limited resources so he arrived in Philadelphia with only five dollars in his pocket. He managed to find enough work (and probably a scholarship) to continue his education, but business studies didn't fascinate him so he changed his direction to medicine after graduation in 1899. At Wharton he had four outstanding years of varsity football and was picked by Water Camp for the All-American Team of 1899. In track he set a shot-put world record in 1898 with 43 feet 8½ inches. It was in the Intercollegiates that he became friendly with Grant and Orton.

He was able to participate fully in team athletics, was president of his class, and still maintained a full curriculum in medical school from which he graduated in 1901. He interned in surgery at St. Lukes Hospital in New York, and then back at the Pennsylvania Hospital in Philadelphia from 1904 to 1906. Sterling College awarded him an honorary M.A. in 1905. He participated as an equal founder and one-third owner of Camp Tecumseh.

His deep Christian faith and a sense of service inspired him to renounce a money-making life as a surgeon in Philadelphia and instead led him to seek a way in which he could make a more significant contribution to mankind. He accepted a challenge by the Christian Association of the University (of which he had been president) to go to China in 1906 and found great medical needs there.

Shortly after his return he married Helen Newpher and together they went off to China in 1907. After serving six years in Canton where he built a medical school for Canton Christian College, he moved on in 1912 to the Medical College of St. Johns University in Shanghai, first as Professor of Surgery and then as Dean. Thirty years later, in 1942, the Japanese occupation forced his return to Philadelphia, but he went back to China from 1946 to 1948. The Communist takeover forced his return to the United States.

Dr. McCracken died on February 15, 1962.

The McCrackens had six daughters and two sons. The first son, Dr. Josiah McCracken, Jr. was

Mike Murphy in 1906

Senior varsity players McCracken (left) and Hare in the football uniform of the day

4

George W. Orton, track star of the University of Toronto in 1893 at the age of 20. He was recruited by Mike Murphy in 1895 and set a new mile record at Penn that same year.

at Tecumseh from 1931 to 1938. Currently a Trustee, his three sons have been at Tecumseh: J.C. McCracken III from 1949 to 1955, Lawrence Lee from 1952 to 1960 (later an Air Force Academy graduate), and Bruce from 1958 to 1986. The second son, Stewart, was at Tecumseh during the 1930s and his son, James, was a counselor in 1988.

George Washington Orton – Canadian Endurance Runner

The flat farm country of Ontario in the small community of Strathroy was the birthplace of George W. Orton on January 10, 1873. Parents Oliver H. and Mary Orton brought forth a lad who was destined to be called (by the Sports Editor of the *Public Ledger* in 1923) "the premier American track athlete of all time, having 17 championships to his credit." As a boy he had spinal meningitis which crippled him. His father forced him to make extra efforts to regain strength and agility by having him walk behind a buggy on his way to school as far as he could each day.

In a newspaper interview Orton said: "I guess I am a development of my own ambition. I began to run when a boy and used to race with all the boys my age in my Canadian home. I found many who could beat me at the races, but as soon as the race became long I killed off all my adherents. This taught me that distance running was evidently my forte and I practiced this continually."

He studied at the Guelph Collegiate Institute (Canada) and then at the University of Toronto where he graduated second in his class of 1893 with a major in modern languages. While at Toronto he joined the Toronto LaCrosse Club in which he continued to run. The Canadian mile and the American mile championships were his in 1892. He repeated these in 1893 and added championships in the two-mile run, and the cross-country races. In other meets as an international competitor, he won championships in Canada, England, Germany, Holland, and Belgium. King Leopold I of Belgium gave him a trophy for his running achievements.

The University of Pennsylvania and the New York Athletic Club had the benefit of his talents while he continued his graduate school studies resulting in a Ph.D. at the age of twenty-three. Graduate students were eligible to join college teams. He was also a whiz at foreign languages.

In 1896 Orton started teaching languages at Eastham Academy in Philadelphia, then spent a year at the Blight School in 1901, and the following year went to Episcopal Academy. With his entrepreneurial ambition he moved to become the first principal of Banks Preparatory School, also in Philadelphia, and then back to Episcopal Academy where he coached track and taught until 1913. The Athletic Association of the University of Pennsylvania called him to be Manager of Publicity and Graduate Coach of Track and Cross-Country Teams about 1914. Training Penn men for Olympic competition was his forte. He introduced ice hockey to the Penn athletic program and played himself until 1934. Another of his contributions to school sports was the promotion of the Penn Relays.

In his personal life he married Edith Wayne Martin of Montreal in 1898, and they had three daughters. However, the marriage ended in divorce in 1932.

We have the impression that Doc Orton, as Alex Grant used to call him, was more interested in the business aspects of Camp Tecumseh than Grant. This may have been a good balance which helped keep the camp solvent while it was struggling to meet all the expenses during the early years.

The partnership between Grant and Orton gradually deteriorated, and Grant bought out Orton's half of Tecumseh on June 14, 1924, with Alex Grant becoming the sole director, able to steer the camp as he had dreamed since 1903.

Orton wrote three books for boys about life at "Camp Pontiac" (which was really Camp Tecumseh) in the 1910-1914 period. They were titled: *Bob Hunt at Camp Pontiac, Bob Hunt, Senior Camper,* and *Bob Hunt in Canada.*

George W. Orton died June 25, 1958, in Laconia, New Hampshire, at the age of eighty-five.

Alexander Grant — Seeker of the Best in Every Boy

Oneida, Ontario, Canada, was the birthplace of Alexander Grant on April 16, 1874. He was a P.K. (preacher's kid) with the Reverend Alexander Grant (Scotch descent) and Anna Hudson (Irish descent) as strict Presbyterian parents. Eventually there were six children in the parsonage of the Knox Presbyterian Church in St. Mary's Ontario. It was a different world where Sundays were for rest and reading and stores were closed. There was no card playing, no dancing, and no alcoholic beverages ever. Alex had two brothers, William Harvey and Richard, and three sisters, Julia, Anna Murray, and Janet Douglas.

Growing up in this large family gave Alex some ideals of family life which often led him in later life to speak of the assembled camp as "The Tecumseh Family." Each camper was expected to share and serve to build community spirit. The tradition now continues in "Founder's Week" service projects.

Running as a sport interested him, judging by his track record at the University of Toronto which he attended for only one year. In Canada he held the half-mile, the one-mile, and the five-mile championships.

He probably had to take some time out to earn money for college since he did not enter the University of Pennsylvania until age twenty-three in 1897. For four years in a row he won the one-mile run and American championship; he won the American steeplechase, the two-mile championship twice; and held the 1500-meter record for twenty years. He was on the Penn track team from 1897 until 1901 when he received his A.B. degree, followed by a Master of Arts in 1902. His major was European History although he later taught English. At Penn he became friends with William Lingelbach, Professor of History, whose son was later active as a boy, then a counselor, and finally a Charter Trustee of Camp Tecumseh.

During his high-school days, "Alex first saw Mabel Delhenty skating on a winter day in St. Mary's. She was about seventeen, was very pretty, a brunette with high color and pansy blue eyes, and

Alex told a friend who was with him that he had just seen the girl he was going to marry." Over a period of years he kept up correspondence with her, and the year of the 1900 Olympics they became engaged. With a busy life at college and financial problems of getting Camp Tecumseh started, he had to defer marriage until June 15, 1908. Five days later Alex Grant bought a 200 x 300 foot lot on the point with 2.6 acres, and probably erected a tent there for his wife. We do know that Mabel became pregnant and spent the summer of 1911 in a tent prior to his building a house. What a way for a wife to begin! There was no road to the site, an outdoor privy, and access only by rowboat or canoe back to the camp dock. Phyllis was born in October 1911 and Eleanor (always known as "Eenie") came in spring of 1913.

The family lived in West Philadelphia until the spring of 1914 when they moved to 508 Essex Avenue, Narberth, although Alex had to commute to Episcopal but wanted a non-city environment for the girls.

Grant's first teaching job had been in New York City at the Berkeley School where he was in 1903 when Camp Tecumseh was established. Next he spent a year as a master in the Detroit University School. "It was too provincial for him" so in 1905 he returned to Pennsylvania and taught for three years at the Hill School in Pottstown, where his lifelong friendship with George Robins (Wolfeboro Camp) began. From Hill he returned to Philadelphia, first to the Phillips Brooks School, then to Delancey School, and finally to Episcopal in 1914 where he remained for the rest of his life as an English teacher. Not surprisingly he also served as track coach from 1914 to 1924. Many counselors were recruited from the Episcopal faculty including Wagner, Shover, Doolittle, McClelland, Davis, Ortlepp, Tabor, Drexel, and Brennan in the years prior to 1948.

Tragedy struck on March 20, 1920, when Mabel died from a heart complication, leaving him with two small daughters, Phyllis, nine, and Eenie, seven. What to do? By fall he had decided to marry Lydia R., a distant cousin from the past, a maiden lady living in Vancouver, B.C. Said Phyllis, "In October 1920 they were married. I think it was a marriage of convenience for both . . . She left in June of 1921 for Vancouver before camp started and that was the last we saw of her."

Alex Grant was a man of many interests. An avid reader of biographies, this hobby gave him lots of anecdotes. He played the piano by ear, and enjoyed classical piano. Flowers and gardening were his forte, and raising cows for a dairy one of his skills. He was a student of the Bible and shared many of the classical historical chapters in his evening and Sunday devotions, but as some boys noted, left out the story of King David and the sexy Bathsheba!

Taking care of yourself and developing a strong body by regular exercise, as well as a keen intellect were stressed. "Living as a fine art" was the way he put it. True Tecumseh boys do not smoke, drink or gamble, was his precept.

Ed Stanley (CT 1926-1936) and now a Trustee, wrote:

"Another recollection I have of Mr. Grant is the kindly way in which he lectured us on our personal behavior and conduct, and I am sure many of us will never forget his warning with respect to drinking liquor, which he referred to as 'putting varnish in your engine.' To this day at parties where 'spirits' are being served I still run into former campers who voice the old caution to one another, perhaps still feeling a little guilty over violating his instructions."

The earliest camp brochures made it very clear that "THE USE OF TOBACCO IN ANY FORM IS FORBIDDEN AT CAMP TECUMSEH." He felt very strongly about this, and confronted the faculty at the Episcopal Academy suggesting that smoking during faculty meetings should be prohibited for the benefit of non-smokers. Headmaster Greville Haslam ruled against him. Because of this and other personality conflicts between the two men, Mr. Grant decided that his plan to turn over Camp Tecumseh to the Episcopal Academy should be changed to making it an independent organization. Despite this earlier friction, the two men later became good friends.

The Hollingsworth farm in 1903, some twenty years before its acquisition by Tecumseh's founders, had only a single story.

The Camp Acquires A Home

The close friendship of McCracken, Orton, and Grant in track events continued during summers after they had been recruited as counselors for Camp Idlewild, a boys' camp on Lake Winnipesaukee, located on Cow Island about four miles from where Tecumseh is now.

The Dick brothers, teachers from Massachusetts, had founded Idlewild in 1891. During their thirty years of operation no woman was ever permitted on the island, and in that remote location swimming in the nude was the practice. These ideas obviously appealed to our three founders, because they became embedded in the Tecumseh philosophy for years.

The three track stars liked the Idlewild experience and sought a site to start a boys' camp of their own. Fortunately the old Moultonboro Poor Farm was for sale. It included a rundown cape farmhouse (which is now the Lodge) with its attached dormitory and a cow barn nearby, over one hundred acres of land, and nearly a mile of lakefront including a natural sand beach in a cove with some seclusion. It extended from what we know as Grant's Point northerly to just beyond the Junior Pagodas.

The farmhouse was erected c. 1778 by Sanborn Chandler who had purchased the land from Jonathan Moulton in 1777, one of the original proprietors who had been given a land grant during British times, and for whom the *Town of Moultonborough* (original spelling) was named. The waterfront extended further out then since the natural lake level was sixteen feet lower before the dam was built in 1805 at Lakeport making Winnipesaukee as we know it today.

In 1839 the town bought it for $1400 and converted it to a Poor Farm for both poor people and the mentally ill. Some had to be restrained since no suitable medications were then available.

The town tore down the small end section toward the lake (the roof line can still be seen inside the Lodge) and added the large room now used for assembly. This was divided into smaller rooms. Underneath were some cells for mentally unstable and violent persons. This was maintained as the Moultonboro Poor Farm until the late 1890s, when the inmates were moved and the farm rented to the George family. A letter from one of the George girls who lived there said: "I remember barred cells in one area and I was afraid of the iron bars. I think they must have been there to control the unruly ones." One of these cell doors still remains in the corner of the Lodge.

Then on December 3, 1898, the town sold the property to Alvin G. Wentworth and Alvin F. Wentworth for $2500. The deed says "containing one hundred acres, more or less." The two islands were not part of the original deal.

We think that the Wentworths bought it for the lumber, for in their deed to McCracken and Grant of New York City, and Orton of Philadelphia on July 16, 1903, they reserved "all the timber standing . . . twelve inches through at the butt and upwards except a small clump of pine . . . near the south end of the beach . . ." The price was not disclosed; but two days after the purchase, the three men took out a mortgage from Alvin G. Wentworth for $1700. Perhaps this was to obtain some working capital to start the camp. This loan was paid off on October 31, 1908.

As we look back today from our perspective of ninety years later, we can only marvel that the founders discovered such a perfect spot for their cherished enterprise.

2

The Dream Becomes Reality

1900 – 1909

The First Years, 1903-1905

RECRUITING the first boys for a new summer camp was a real challenge. There was no record of past experience and no alumni to use for references. What parent wanted to send a twelve-year-old boy away for ten weeks to a remote campsite in New Hampshire to be run by three young men not quite thirty years old? Further, the place was virtually unreachable except by an overnight train trip, and finally a steamboat to the beach. Automobile travel was rare, it was 415 miles from Philadelphia, and road maps and route signs hadn't been thought of yet. A flat tire every one hundred miles was commonplace.

Nevertheless, McCracken, Orton, and Grant had lots of character references, and managed to get nine boys for 1903. Orton was teaching at the Episcopal Academy, and probably did most of the recruiting. Later he ran advertisements in the *Penn Charter Magazine*. Delancey School was close to Episcopal in town and we know a number of Delancey boys came over the years. Grant was in New York at the Berkeley School in 1903 and McCracken was busy in medical school with little secondary school contact, although he remained president of the camp until 1905.

What did the pioneer boys find? They came by train to the Weirs. Then they boarded a steamboat to the Camp Tecumseh beach where they had to jump overboard into shallow water about twenty feet from shore since there was no dock. Walking up the hill they came to a decrepit old building with broken windows and some siding falling off. This was where they would eat. There was neither electricity nor a telephone on the property. The

---

World Events of the Decade

1900	Boxer uprising in China.	1905	International Workers of the World founded.
1901	President William McKinley assassinated.	1906	Earthquake destroys San Francisco.
1902	U.S. acquires control of Panama Canal.	1907	U.S. Government budget reaches $1 billion.
1903	Ford Motor Company established.	1908	First woman arrested for smoking in public.
1904	Russo-Japanese War breaks out.	1909	Robert E. Perry reaches the North Pole.

10

kitchen was part of the original farmhouse (now the office end of the Lodge), and dining tables were set up inside. There was a porch on the lake end of the building.

The boys were also confronted with the fact that insane people had been incarcerated in cells, some of which were still under the Lodge. Ghost stories became part of Tecumseh's tradition.

Mr. Grant and Doc Orton always had a medical doctor as one of the counselors. Very early in the ten-week session, the doctor would examine each boy and measure his height, weight, and arm and leg muscles. Then at the end of the season these measurements would be repeated, and the growth shown on a card which the boy could take home.

This rundown farmhouse which eventually became the Lodge was available at a very low price in 1903.

In 1904, Tecumseh's second year, the entire camp numbered twenty-nine.

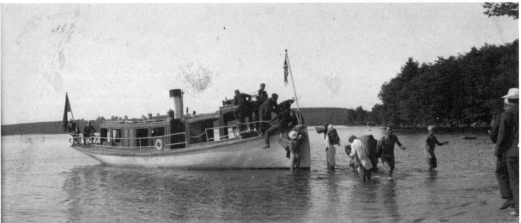

Upon arrival at camp on the Iroquois *in 1904, wading was a requirement.*

The Dream Becomes Reality

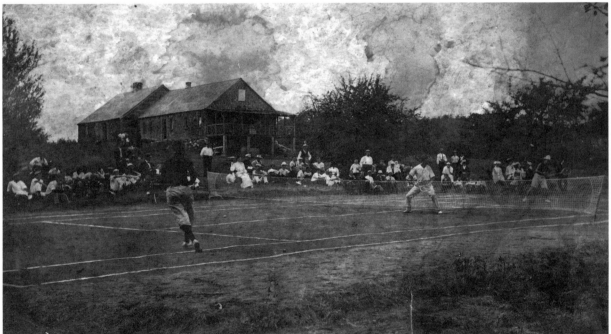

Tennis match on Tecumseh Day in 1904. Note the new porch on the Lodge in the background.

Camp Tecumseh

*The start of a race on Moultonborough Neck Road in 1905.
Alexander Grant is at the right.*

*Recipients of awards for performance and sportsmanship on
Tecumseh Day, 1905*

*Dining on the Lodge porch in 1905. Alex Grant is at the left and
Cole Stanton at the right with forty-three boys beyond.*

The Dream Becomes Reality

Ready for an overnighter with blanket roll packs in 1905

These early years were a real adventure and included plenty of physical work helping to get some places for sports established. A crude baseball backstop was built from scrap lumber and several birch tree poles. Down by the waterfront a gymnastics bar was erected using two poles supporting a horizontal pipe about seven feet above the ground.

One "tennis court" was laid out about two hundred feet from the present Trunk Room on the flat field area toward the lake. It was grass covered and not very level, and there was no fencing to stop the balls. The following year in 1904, an area was leveled, and a clay court built on which tennis matches were held for Tecumseh Day. Still there were no fencing or backstops for the balls! The present location for the tennis courts next to the Lodge came a few years later.

Running events were held on Moultonboro Neck Road which was gravel at that time. Only an occasional horse and wagon or a farm cart pulled by a team of oxen would pass. The mail was deliv-

ered by horse and wagon.

In 1903 the next property to the north which we know as the Hollingsworth Farm did not belong to Tecumseh. Without this farm, there was no place for the cows to graze except around the Lodge or down near the beachfront. Cows were a part of life, and cow "pies" a constant hazard.

From the beginning mountain trips and lake activities were scheduled. There were rigorous rules for swimming safety and no one was allowed in the water until the "All In" signal was given by Mr. Grant, or a counselor was present.

The barn of the old Poor Farm was partly cleaned out and became known as the Trunk Room because each boy who came had a trunk shipped by train and brought over on the steamboat from the Weirs. The trunks were stored in rows on the ground floor since no lockers were yet available.

Mr. Grant did the meal planning and food purchasing and hired the cooks. Usually the chief cook was a man from one of the private schools from

Alex Grant shows a city boy how it's done, 1905.

The Dream Becomes Reality

16

A special horse-drawn rig carried war canoes overland to race sites in the area in 1906.

Camp Tecumseh

Loading the grub wagon with blanket rolls and food preparatory to a mountain hike

which the boys were recruited. It is doubtful that a garden was established in 1903 but certainly a farmer was recruited. The farmer was to be a general caretaker, build needed facilities, buy cows to develop a dairy, do the plowing, and start a garden in the spring.

There were two objectives in having an active farm. One was to become as self-sufficient in food as possible to minimize costs; the other, equally important, was to enable city boys to experience some farm life with gardens and animals to which most had never been exposed.

Much of the 110-acre Tecumseh property had been lumbered a few years before it was acquired, thus the trees were small and there was an abundance of brush. Lots of clearing and cleaning-up was done to develop tent sites and paths through the woods. The cuttings were hauled to the beachfront on a haywagon and piled up as the basis for some huge bonfires which became an annual tradition.

Bald Knob in the Ossipee Mountains was a favorite destination; by canoe to Melvin Village then on to the summit with a possible overnight on top.

The Dream Becomes Reality

18

The wood-fired cook stove with roasts ready for the oven in 1909

By 1904 the camp had grown to twenty-nine boys and counselors. There was still enough room in the old farmhouse to eat inside. This year a simple dock was built and a small bathhouse about eight by ten feet was added. The steamboat *Iroquois* could now discharge boys, freight, and trunks right onto the pier!

More improvements came in 1905 including the large stone fireplace at one end of the Lodge, and a side porch (veranda) on the side toward the Trunk Room. With forty-two at camp, meals were now served on the new porch. Cole Stanton, a teacher from the Pomfret School in Connecticut, joined the counselor staff. He was in charge of the Junior Campus until 1911 and became a lifelong friend of Mr. Grant. Cooking was his forte, and he often went on mountain trips and prepared great meals while the boys hiked.

A regular tennis court was now in place with a clay surface but still no fences. Tennis matches and baseball games with Melvin Village were held on Tecumseh Day in 1905 when spectators came from nearby areas and many parents visited by boat.

By 1905 founder Josiah McCracken had finished his medical courses and was now heavily involved as an intern at the Pennsylvania Hospital in Philadelphia so that his time for Camp Tecumseh was very limited. When the Christian Association at the University asked him to consider medical missionary work in China in 1905, he decided to give up his active relationship with Tecumseh. On December 21, 1905, he sold his one-third share to Grant and Orton for $3000, taking back a mortgage for the full sale price, with a provision that the debt would be reduced to $1500 if all insurance payments were made on time until the 1910 maturity date. He feared Grant and Orton might cancel the insurance when money was tight!

The next major addition came in 1906 with construction of the dining hall and kitchen plus a separate ice house behind the kitchen. In the winter when the lake ice was about 18 inches thick, the farmers cut blocks with a large ice saw and hauled them on a sledge, drawn by a team of horses, up to the ice house. There they were stored

The kitchen storeroom. In 1908 flour was $5.50 a barrel, cornflakes were $2.90 for a case of 36, and pears were $.58 per #10 can.

The original barn of the Poor Farm in 1906 — now and for many years the Trunk Room

The Dream Becomes Reality

20

with sawdust around the outside for insulation, and a layer of sawdust on top. This would be enough to ice the kitchen refrigerators for the entire summer, and the practice continued until 1952.

By 1908 the camp had grown to a total of seventy persons. No financial records were preserved but we know that the tuition was $175 for ten weeks. In 1908 the camp finally paid off the $1700 mortgage taken out in 1903, and in 1910 the Mc-Cracken mortgage was retired.

Next came the new beach house constructed for the 1909 season. In 1992 this still looks about the same in design and location, although it was badly damaged in the hurricane of 1938 and replaced.

Reveille to start the day in 1908; a call to the lakefront for calisthenics

A nostalgic look at the well, icehouse, and dining hall in 1907

The Iroquois *picks up a group at Tecumseh dock in 1909.*

Mail delivery on Moultonborough Neck Road in 1906

The Dream Becomes Reality

22

Trunk room with trunks, 1909

Two boys, one pickerel, and one bass, 1909

We don't know how Grant and Orton financed all the improvements during these early years. Carlos Cardeza, who was first there in 1915, thought that Herr Fred Meyer may have helped Camp Tecumseh financially. Meyer served as a counselor for a long time. He had his own tent, a dog named Jack, and is spoken of highly throughout the history up to the 1930 period. He had his own launch and frequently towed canoes home from trips to Melvin Village or Adams Mills, now called "Lee's Mills." Having been a worldwide traveler, he showed lantern slides to the camp from time to time. He was obviously a man of considerable resources who shared his time, money, and talents with the Tecumseh family.

By the end of 1909 the camp was well established with enough boys (100) to almost break even and with sufficient facilities to run a full program. The list of forty-one well-known persons who lent their support as references highlights the fine reputation of the camp. This included John Wanamaker, ex-postmaster general of the United States and founder of the Wanamaker store; C.C. Harrison, provost of the University of Pennsylvania; Dr. Floyd W. Tompkins, pastor of Holy Trinity Church, Philadelphia; John C. Bell, ex-district attorney, Philadelphia; Henry L. Geyelin, president of the University of Pennsylvania Athletic Association; and the headmasters of eleven private schools.

Hiking and Canoeing Adventures

The boys of the early years did a lot of hiking and canoeing typified by this description of an adventure on July 24, 1908. This is taken from the "Camp History" written by one boy or counselor each day, and forwarded to each boy's parents weekly in the 1908-1921 period.

July 24th — No setting up drill. After breakfast about 15 fellows took a trip to Mt. Whiteface. The baseball team was at Camp Wachusetts the previous day and had left their canoes and blankets in Center Harbor . . . After dinner (noon) twelve fellows walked to Center Harbor to bring back the canoes left there. After a six-and-a-half mile walk we arrived at Center Harbor. We got sodas, ice cream

In 1910 the Lodge had a battery-operated bell on the roof to call staff by code. Grant is seated in the middle of the foreground group and Orton is at the right with hands in pockets.

1909 Council. Standing: Charles Wharton, Dr. Carl Steinke, Eddie Bothwell, R. Hansel, and Pop Ehmke. Seated in back: Sig Spaeth, Ned Bixby, Ludwig Lewis, and Cole Stanton. Seated in center: Alex Grant, and George Orton. Seated in front: John Alexander, unidentified, Eames Stouffer, unidentified, and Ernie Murdoch

Herr Meyer and the Woox's in 1909. Top row: Wood, Edward L. Davis, Heath Bannard, Rankin, and Ludwig Lewis; Middle row: Howard McCall, Herr Meyer (Honorary President), and Charlie Synder; Bottom row: Eames Stouffer, James Gould, and Charles Cheston

The Dream Becomes Reality

24

and crackers and candy and then started for camp in the war canoes. [Note: A war canoe could hold up to 18 people]. We had a full load with the blankets, bats and other things. The wind was coming up stronger all the time and the waves splashed over the bow and soaked everybody so Mr. Chaplin decided to make land and walk home. When we reached shore we took out the blankets and carried the canoes out of the water. It was already dark . . . In about a mile we reached camp. We went to the dining room and found the baseball team there. We had a cold supper, and then bed and a good sleep. The ball team had to sleep without their blankets. By L.C. Murdock.

Jottings

Mr. Grant the Teacher

One insight into Mr. Grant's way of teaching is shown in the history entry for July 21, 1908:

. . . We then had our luncheon and some of the fellows went and picked berries for pies . . . After supper the gluttons of the camp headed by Mr. Grant (not saying that Mr. Grant is one) stayed on and ate pie while the gentlemen stayed out and watched them feed. P.S. Those . . . gentlemen included those who did not care to pick berries in the woods.

With no electricity in 1909, all laundry was done in this hand-cranked machine, later turned into a tank for Tecumseh punch.

On the bar by the lake in the old apple orchard, 1909

Winter and cows at Tecumseh in 1909, when the trunk room was the cow barn

After this episode there were many more berry picker volunteers that year when trips were announced. Mr. Grant did not beg for work to be done but his messages were always clear.

Tutoring Program

A tutoring program was instituted for boys needing extra instruction in school subjects. Recruitment of counselors recognized the need to get coverage for this. Parents paid on an hourly basis.

Tutors for 1905: George W. Orton: English, French, German, Latin; Philip T. White: Mathematics and English; Garfield Weed: Mathematics, Latin, and Greek; Richard E. Danielson: English, Latin, and Greek; C. Pomeroy Fiske: Mathematics, English, German; C.E. Stanton: Greek, Latin, French, German, and Music; B.M. Fontaine: Greek, Latin, French, and English; W.R. McCullough: English branches; Walter Whittlesley: English and History; and F.J. Richardson: Maine guide for canoe trip.

A Typical Day

A typical day began with a bugle wake-up call followed by setting-up exercises near the beach, then a quick dip and breakfast. The daily schedule was posted, usually very early in the morning, by Mr. Grant. This would show what each age group was doing and list counselors in charge of trips. Two were also assigned to the beach.

A noon swim for the entire camp followed the morning sports, with the main meal of the day about 12:30 P.M. In the afternoon there were more sports, another swim, and a light supper which often included prunes, one of Mr. Grant's favorite health foods. There were some pickup games after supper, then everyone assembled for vespers or a brief inspirational reading or remarks, prayers, taps, and bed. This was abbreviated to P.P.T.B.—*Prunes, Prayers, Taps, and Bed.*

Athletic Competitions

Competitions with other camps were started and rivalries continued over the years. One of the earliest was with Camp Pemigewasset which still continues. Other camps mentioned in this early period include Camp Wachusetts and the Harvard Engineering Camp.

3

Busy Years at Tecumseh

1910 – 1919

THE DECADE STARTED with the basic building needs met and a reputation for providing boys with a balanced program so that many returned the following year. Top attention to sports of all kinds and frequent competitions with neighboring camps and towns continued. It was a time for recruitment of some long-term leadership including Walter and Ralph Johnson, Joe Lorraine, Mike Dorizas, and Wallace Arnold—men who served the camp with the ideals Grant wanted. It was a time for hiking, mountain climbing, and canoeing trips that challenged every boy. Trips started from camp on foot or by canoe and went long distances without using cars or trucks, real adventures that are not possible today because of crowded roads.

Reaching Camp Tecumseh

Getting to Camp Tecumseh was an adventure in itself, as Alex Grant described in a letter to parents in 1914:

The party will leave Broad Street Station, Pennsylvania Railroad, on a special car attached to the 2 P.M. train for New York, and will go to the downtown station in New York and walk from there to the Fall River Line Pier, only two blocks away. They will reach Boston at seven o'clock the next morning, take breakfast at the Essex Hotel, and take the 9:30 train from the North Station to Weirs. Lunch will be served at Hotel Weirs and immediately afterwards the party will leave for camp on the Governor Endicott. They should reach camp about 3:30 P.M.

World Events of the Decade

1910	Japan annexes Korea.		1915	U.S. Coast Guard established.
1911	Roald Amundsen reaches South Pole.		1916	Battle of Verdun.
1912	*Titanic* sinks, 1595 drowned out of 2340.		1917	United States declares war on Germany.
1913	Ford Model T assembly line opens.		1918	World War I ends, November 11th.
1914	Germany starts World War I.		1919	Prohibition Amendment (18th) ratified.

A well-dressed group waiting for the train home at The Weirs in 1912

27

The best time for a pump house visit was when the paddle came out of the ice cream freezer.

By 1912 a silo had been added to the Trunk Room and an addition was under way to house the cows.

Busy Years at Tecumseh

28

Costs were: berth on the boat, $1.00; dinner on boat, $1.00; breakfast at Hotel Essex, $0.75; chair on train from Boston to Weirs, $0.55; lunch at Weirs, $0.50; and round-trip boat ticket to camp, $0.75. Total $4.55, excluding train tickets. The fee for the ten-week season at camp was $200, tutoring extra at moderate rates.

These were more formal times and boys dressed in knickers, coats, shirts, neckties, and caps for the trip.

Adjusting to Camp Life

For boys often for the first time away from home, there were some tough adjustments to make. Homesickness always hit a few but Mr. Grant knew how to handle this. He would tell parents that they should not call the camp during the first week, and they should not agree with a son who wants to go home if he calls.

Some of the adjustments included nude bathing—a new experience for most and soon part of a healthy outlook when you were there for awhile. A day or two after camp began the Blue-

Gray team elections were held. The entire camp was divided into two teams at each age level for an all-season series of competitive sports events. The new boys were often picked *last* since about half of the boys had been in camp the previous summer and the team captain knew who were the better athletes. After a week it was rare that a boy wasn't happy and wanted to stay. After ten weeks all were sorry to see the summer end, and new friendships had developed that often lasted a lifetime.

The Saguenay Club and Camp Iroquois

From 1910 to 1919 Grant remained as president and Orton as secretary-treasurer. Orton, however, wanted some projects of his own so in 1911 he started the Saguenay Club as a partnership with Libe Washburn and Camp Tecumseh. It was organized "to give business men, college men, and ex-Tecumseh boys a chance to get into the Canadian wilds for fishing and hunting trips." The club was included in the Camp Tecumseh brochure up to 1916, after which no further mention was made of it.

Women approaching – everybody in the water

Camp Tecumseh

The next venture of Doc Orton's about 1917 was to open a family camp and a junior camp for girls named Camp Iroquois, on a site on Moultonboro Neck Road. Doc Orton secured Dr. Ann Tompkins Gibson, a surgeon, daughter of the Reverend Floyd Tompkins of Holy Trinity Episcopal Church in Philadelphia, as director of the girls' camp there. She carried on this activity under the name Singing Eagle Lodge when it was moved to Squam Lake a few years later. Camp Tecumseh had many dances with Singing Eagle Lodge up to 1975 when it closed. Alex Grant and Doc Ann had numerous common ideals and were good friends.

Strained relationships began to develop between Grant and Orton, perhaps because Orton was involved with other activities. A personal note from Orton to Grant in 1915 stated: "The camp will not be a success until we can get our boys each season without so much effort. We must change our attitude one towards the other or dissolve the partnership." To which Grant wrote at the bottom: "and towards the camp?" By 1913 Orton had left teaching at Episcopal Academy and was coaching track at Penn and still living in the city. Grant was farsighted enough to see Philadelphians gradually moving to the suburbs; the Episcopal Academy moved to Merion in 1921. Thus his Narberth location to which Orton had once objected, was actually better for recruiting boys.

Grant's objective of having a lot of the food for the camp produced on the property was becoming a reality. More land was needed so he leased some fields from John H. Morrison on the Neck, and was making plans for a barn in 1915 although it was never built. In 1911 he had a silo added to the Trunk Room and a side shed addition for the cows. In 1919 the herd improved with the addition of a bull named "Tecumseh Reliance Pontiac."

Busy Years at Tecumseh

One city boy plus one calf equals bliss.

Herr Meyer, a retired gentleman, a fondly remembered counselor, and one who may have helped finance Tecumseh in the early years.

Part of the herd of twenty cows, prime source of plentiful ice cream on the daily menu

A tough match on some hard ground in 1912

Camp Tecumseh

The dining hall in 1914; one hundred and four boys and twenty-six counselors dining in style on white tablecloths

31

Nine years after Tecumseh's founding the road to the beach was still stony and the trees were small.

Busy Years at Tecumseh

The original Point House, built in 1914 by Alex Grant for his family, was moved to its present location in the 1950s. It had no door on the screened porch for the safety of his family.

Mabel Delhenty Grant, married in 1908 to Alex Grant, with their daughter Phyllis in 1914

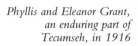

Phyllis and Eleanor Grant, an enduring part of Tecumseh, in 1916

Church at Melvin Village

On Sundays in good weather the whole camp went to Melvin Village to church.

Listen my children and you shall hear
The day dawned cloudy but soon grew clear,
We paddled in boats to Melvin Town,
And heard the sermon of Brother Brown.

At Haley's and Caverley's we stopped
And guzzled eats until we nearly dropped,
In war canoes we paddled home
(How do you like this doggone pome).

The entire Tecumseh Navy was used for the Melvin voyage, with assigned boats for all. The boat list for July 28, 1912, included 20 boys each in three war canoes, 10 in a junior war canoe, 3 or 4 each in 10 regular canoes, and 4 each in 5 boats. This was a total of 20 water craft, and 113 boys and counselors. It is about three miles to Melvin Village by boat and fourteen by gravel road.

At the Melvin Community Church ". . . the Minister preached as usual an able sermon, making no unpleasant remarks about Capitalism and thus keeping us in good spirits."

Before and after church, the boys stopped at Haley's Ice Cream Store near the main dock at Melvin. In the 1930s this place was known as the Gray Birches. Today it is a residence.

Camp Tecumseh

Program

COMIC IMITATIONS
DIALECT SONGS
BANJO SELECTIONS
HAND BELLS SOLOS
OCOREINA
XYLOPHONE
WHISTLING
STORIES

In Music.

In Fun.

JOE LORRAINE THE MANUFACTURER OF BROAD SMILES

July 18-1914

Oxen on the Moultonborough Neck Road in 1914

The store and post office in the Lodge, 1915

Busy Years at Tecumseh

BASE BALL
PEARL ST. GROUNDS
SATURDAY, AUGUST 19, 1916
Game Called at 3.00 P. M.
CAMP TECUMSEH
VS.
LACONIA

Camp Tecumseh is the largest summer camp in New Hampshire and they have a crack ball team and are coming over with a big crowd of Lake visitors to see them win.

A band concert will be given before and during the game. Both teams will parade the streets starting from Depot Square at 2 P. M.

Laconia will have McPherson, Young, Pease, Sheehan, Clare, Teft, McCarthy, Jewell, Johnson, Lougee and Buzzell.

JOSEPH H. KILLOURHY, Umpire

ADMISSION - - - - **GENTS 25C**
LADIES 15c   CHILDREN 15c   GRAND STAND 10c
                    SPACE FOR AUTOMOBILES
        Please Post.   Printed by the NEWS AND CRITIC, Laconia, N. H.

Camp Tecumseh

Tecumseh's 1904 baseball team included both Grant and Orton.

Future big leaguer Howard John Ehmke at the age of eighteen

Tecumseh plays a local town team in 1905

The Winnipesaukee Baseball League

During this period the Winnipesaukee Baseball League was active with town teams and camp teams participating. Tecumseh had games with Melvin, Wolfeboro, Laconia, and a long list of camps including Harvard Engineering, Wachusetts, Sandy Island, Belknap, Winnisquam, Idlewild, Pemigewasset, Hill, Moosilaukee, Algonquin, Ozark, Woodcrest, and Green Point.

A notable game with Laconia was reported:

Fifteen members of the camp team left for Laconia in canoes towed by Herr Meyer. We were all resolved to give an exhibition which would long be remembered in the Lake City. We did. Everyone was thoroughly soaked in the Broads. We arrived at the Weirs and left as quickly as possible for Laconia (often by trolley car). Here the five

councillors [sic] were entertained at dinner in the Eagle Hotel. In walking around town we discovered flaming [sic] posters of the game describing our team in detail. Out of nine players, all but two were wrong.

Meanwhile the uncouncillored team was keeping Lent at the ball field. Duer dropped his glove in a pig pen, and when he tried to get it, he was assaulted by the ferocious animals. However, as he sleeps between Gould and Morris, he knew how to act and soon made his escape, and in so doing broke the world's record for the high jump, softly alighting on a barbed wire fence . . . at three o'clock the game began. As no one had provided an adding machine we soon lost count of the errors and runs. Finally the game was ended and we had made an impression that will never be erased—even the cows came out on the field and tried to chase us off.

Busy Years at Tecumseh

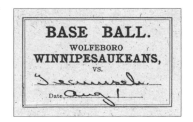

BASE BALL.
WOLFEBORO
WINNIPESAUKEANS,
VS.
Tecumseh
Date Aug 1

Ticket, circa 1910

Entertainment in 1914. Alex Grant is standing behind the pianist.

36

Grant and Orton on the dock, and the Tecumseh family of eighty-nine in 1915

Camp Tecumseh

Drama at the Lodge in 1916 was illuminated by kerosene lanterns surrounded by pine boughs

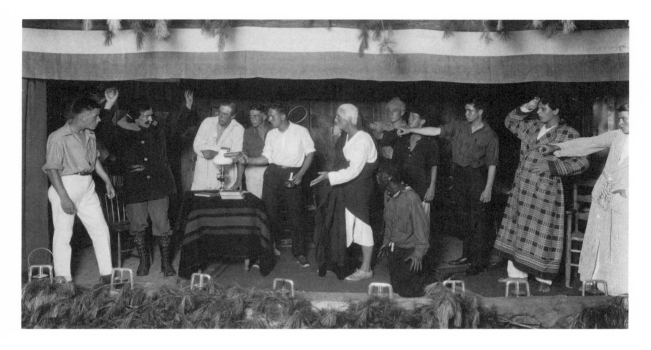

Ralph and Walter Johnson

About 1916 the arrival of two brothers, Ralph and Walter Johnson, was the start of a long-term relationship. Walter was Princeton 1915 and always enthusiastically interested in the arts, drama, and music. Ralph, an engineer from Stevens Tech, was naturally more mechanically oriented.

Walter was a creator of skits and musicals for the weekly Saturday night performances which were usually held in the Lodge. Pine branches were hung from the rafters, and stage lighting was with *kerosene lanterns surrounded by pine boughs*. Why the place never burned down is amazing. For the music a piano was rented in Boston. A letter from Cole Stanton in 1911 to Grant states: "My train was late . . . Steinway and Chickering Stores wanted $30 so I finally ordered an Ives and Pond upright to be sent up by freight at once. Their lowest term for renting is 3 months—price $18, so I told them to go ahead."

Walter introduced the idea of an outdoor stage which gave more room and townspeople and summer residents were invited. On Friday, August 3, 1917,

This evening the woodland theater was officially opened. . . . The stage and scenery were beautifully set off in a small grove of pine trees through which the full moon could be seen shining over the lake. There was an audience of three hundred people seated on chairs and benches beneath the trees. Among the guests were the girls of Camp Iroquois as well as many summer people from the lake and the country people. On the whole it was the greatest dramatic success achieved in the history of camp dramatics. . . . It was over by 10:30 . . . cheers were given for the cast, managers, and especially Walter Johnson.

An earlier attempt at outdoor dramatics on July 15, 1915, had a different ending:

The mighty tent #4 were to give their play in the evening, but just as they were discussing the possibility of rain, the heavens opened their flood gates and washed the piano into the orchestra pit. When the storm passed we all swam to our respective campuses and dove into bed.

Busy Years at Tecumseh

Mountain Trips

Mountain trips were frequent for all age groups, and many were overnighters. Each boy had two blankets, and a poncho, and made up a blanket roll (probably with blanket safety pins) and whatever personal articles he wished to take provided the weight was less than 15 pounds. The pack frame for the campers didn't exist. All of the packs and the food were loaded on a horse-drawn wagon which set out for the campsite on the road. The boys frequently went by canoe to Adams Mills (now Lee's Mills) and started hiking from there, or they went by steamboat to the Weirs to get the train or trolley car. On reaching the planned campsite, they slept on the ground without tents. If a rainstorm came up, then they ran for shelter in a barn, or shed or sometimes rented a room in a nearby hotel if they had the 50 cents required. Occasionally one or two boys would pay the 50 cents, and then a crowd would come up the fire escape into their room after dark.

On August 19-23, 1912, the Mt. Washington Trip took place. (Abstracts of a long report.)

Twenty-three of us were up at 5:30 cheered by the distant rumble of thunder and the sight of heavy black clouds. . . . Herr Meyer took us by the good ship Tecumseh to Adams Mills—a small metropolis, four miles up the lake. By seven o'clock we were on the road. Tamworth was our first destination. . . . In that ancient city ice cream is to be procured—and root beer, the delicate flavor of which will not soon be forgotten. The grub wagon with its precious burden (Chas. Wharton and little Heath) came quite late . . . so lunch at two o'clock. At nightfall we stopped at the Piper House, a fashionable resort nine miles from Tamworth en route for Jackson. . . . We slept in open fields. Tuesday dawned fair, and with sore and reluctant feet we strolled to Intervale, our lunching place. Edson, Riley and someone else got a long lift in an automobile. . . . On to Jackson.

Wednesday we were awakened by Dr. Orton falling over a fence in his efforts to get some firewood. We walked 12 miles Wed. to the Glen House. . . . Just after supper a dark looking thunderstorm was seen descending from the mountains. Each man seized his blankets and looked about for a shelter. The Glen House having refused

admittance to their barn, we were forced to take refuge in some smaller buildings, which formerly served as a tollgate. . . . The majority uncomfortably settled themselves on some odds and ends of hay.

The rather inhospitable owner of the property so rudely seized, entered after everyone was fixed for the night and warned all to be very careful as there was some dynamite stored in the loft. An awful silence followed his foreboding words, broken only by the heavy claps of thunder and the ever more brilliant lightning. The storm followed will ever be remembered by those who experienced it. Four of the fellows who slept in the loft near the dynamite seemed inclined to levity, assuring those below that dynamite always blows downward . . . presently the rain began to descend in torrents, the thunder roared and the lightning was vivid. Several saw it jump along the telephone wires some twenty feet away and trembled with horror. Presently above the awful roar of the storm, rose a sweet voice singing steadily "Softly now the light of Day." It was an Edson Bro.—we won't say which but the other one was saying his prayers. Encouraged by this powerful example, all took heart and the night of horror passed at last.

They got to the top of Mt. Washington, then the rains came again with eight miles to go to Crawford's via the Southern Peaks. It kept raining for three hours while they descended.

At Crawford's it was discovered that the train was an hour late; in soaking clothes we at last were borne to North Conway where we had expected to sleep. Meanwhile the

Camp Tecumseh

A stop at Camp Hermance on the Appalachian Trail en route to Mt. Washington

All Tecumseh seniors and intermediates participated in military drill in 1918.

grub wagon captained by the Honorable C. Heath Bannard had made all efforts for our comfort at Conway Center and telegraphed Dr. Orton to that effect. The telegram miscarried and we were stranded five miles from our hot supper, supperless and wet. The grub wagon was summoned and we slept on the soft comfortable platform of the Maine Central station. An occasional express train roaring by ten feet away lent color to our dreams and by its gentle rumble soothed us. The night freights had a peculiar method of blowing off steam, especially attractive. We arose at dawn satisfied that the night had been very pleasant.

Friday was a day of plugging. We had to cover twenty-five miles to reach Adams Mills by five o'clock . . . lunch at Tamworth. . . . About five o'clock the sight of a row of lumber piles was welcome to the foot sore and weary. Herr Meyer was there and behind his good ship we came to camp. We were tired certainly—but still lively as the singing and the cheering showed. The dining room, a good supper, and a real bed where the luxuries that nearly overpowered us that Friday night.

So ended the last trip of the season and the greatest. The distance covered on foot was one hundred and six miles, some of which was the hardest kind of mountain climbing.

Busy Years at Tecumseh

World War I Brings Change

The war in Europe at the end of this decade brought some changes at Tecumseh. In a letter of May 24, 1917, to parents, Dr. Orton said:

We would like to know whether you desire your boy to take part in the military training course that we are giving this year. . . . We have to get various equipment for this work. . . . We ask you to let us know as soon as possible . . .

We have put in a large field of potatoes and we are going to ask the boys to cultivate these. Whatever is made from this work will be given to the Red Cross or some other war charity.

Rifles were obtained and regular military drills were held. Boys did work in the fields, and for years afterwards boys continued to take turns with the vegetable gardens and corn fields with modest pay unless it was a day for all the camp to participate.

With the war over, the camp rules added to the prohibition against tobacco in any form that "No boy at Camp is allowed to have firearms."

So Camp Tecumseh came through the war years with a full complement of boys, and was able to staff with enough older men to run a full program. Now for the twenties!

1919 registration of a Tecumseh launch of special character

The 1916 Council, from, left: standing - second Mike Dorizas, seventh and eighth, Ralph and Walter Johnson; seated starting with fourth: Wallace Arnold, Orton, Grant, and Herr Meyer.

Interior of the pump house by the lake in 1915 with the freezer on the right and water pump at left. Belts were shifted with a baseball bat.

Jottings

Congratulatory Letters

A few portions from letters from four parents to Grant and Orton in 1912 showed the success of the programs:

"My boy writes that he is having the time of his life. He is evidently very happy."

"I want to express to you my approbation of what you are doing. The physical part of it comes as a natural result of an outdoor life, but what especially impressed me was the good moral tone that seems to permeate all the doings in your camp life."

"The association with men and with nature, ought to do much towards making men of them; and that my boy should become a true man is more to me than education or wealth."

"I find my boy much more manly and self-reliant as a result of his summer at Camp Tecumseh."

Historians' Comments

The historians of each day continued to comment on important happenings:

"Platt caught a nice big bullfrog in the evening and presented it to Mr. McKenzie's cot without permission of the owner."

"1910. Mr. Wharton gave us $1/2$ hour of setting up . . . and Tom Finletter celebrated by going in swimming." (Tom Finletter later went to Penn Law School, was Secretary of the Navy under President Truman, and was Ambassador to NATO from 1960–1965.)

"There was no setting up because we had returned from trips." Mr. Grant believed in flexibility and on rainy mornings would have breakfast a half hour later.

July 1912. "At supper Taylor Walthour broke all records by eating 14 hot cakes in the wonderful time of 4 minutes 45 $2/5$ seconds. . . . After supper we had prayers in which the choir extinguished itself."

4

A Successful Blend

1920 – 1929

———

THE DECADE BEGAN with a continuation of the nine-week season begun in 1919, and with the tuition raised to $250. Grant and Orton were still in charge with Grant pushing to improve the food supply by raising more animals and planting bigger vegetable gardens.

We need to look back a bit for perspective. Mr. Grant had built a house in 1914 for his family on a two-and-one-half-acre lot on the lake which he had purchased May 15, 1908. Known as the Point House it was constructed with a screened porch across the front without a door so that his two little girls Phyllis and Eenie would be safe and not venture into the lake. All the meals had to be transported to the Grant family from the camp kitchen down to the lake and then by rowboat or canoe. Grant did not approve of wives of staff eating in the dining hall.

Phyllis and Eenie had a role to play at the Point House which Phyllis described as "Homesick Haven."

We would see a rowboat with a small passenger plying its way toward our dock. Then my father with a woebegone child in tow would disembark to explain to my mother that said child was in need of some TLC. In a few days the acute homesickness would wear off while Eenie and I had this neat little kid to play with. Then he'd go back to camp with occasionally a temporary relapse.

City Boys, Cows and Farm Chores

There were now twenty cows and a bull and a great need for more barn space. In addition the Trunk Room (which was really a barn) had possibilities for other uses if the cows could be moved out. In 1920 Dr. Zachary T. Hollingsworth was

———

World Events of the Decade

1920	U.S refuses to join League of Nations.	1925	Hitler publishes Volume I of *Mein Kampf.*
1921	First radio broadcast of a baseball game.	1926	Goddard fires first liquid fuel rocket.
1922	Stock market "boom" starts after depression.	1927	Lindbergh flies New York to Paris nonstop.
1923	First birth control clinic opens in New York.	1928	Kellogg-Briand Pact, outlawing war, signed.
1924	Hugo Eckener flies dirigible across Atlantic.	1929	U.S. stock market collapses in October.

General View at Camp Tecumseh

Bunny Kinder, Andy Young, Fletcher Nyce, Wooz Supplee and Dave McMullin face the camera near summit of Mt. Lafayette in 1922. Jack and Bill Carney are sitting at the left.

ready to sell his adjacent farm which had an excellent large barn. The farmhouse had been expanded since 1903, the house had been raised, and a new first floor added with porches on the rear and the west end. On November 1, 1920, Alex Grant and George Orton acquired this farm of about 250 acres and made plans for increasing camp enrollment by taking on more seven- and eight-year-olds who at that time were called "Sub-Juniors." (Ten years later they were known as "Junior C's.")

One more property addition was made in 1921 when the two islands were purchased from Dr. Hollingsworth. Mr. Grant prior to this had warned everyone to enjoy the custom of nude bathing for as long as possible; for if the islands fell into non-Tecumseh hands, that meant bathing suits. In the fall of 1920, Dr. Hollingsworth offered to sell the two islands named Jocks and Poplar for $1800. Grant and Orton agreed to buy with settlement to take place the following spring. During the winter Dr. Hollingsworth had the timber cut off the islands, and when April came, he said that the price would only be $400 since he had sold the timber for $1400. Dr. Hollingsworth believed in Tecumseh!

arbor, N. H. 1920.

At this point Mr. Grant decided to form Camp Tecumseh, Incorporated, to which he and his distant wife Lydia conveyed all of the property, including the islands, on April 14, 1925. Perhaps he had to do this to help his financial situation since there could now be additional stockholders. No details are recorded although in the second year Fred J. Doolittle and Walter Johnson became assistant directors of the camp.

With the increased acreage, more edible corn could now be added to the menu. There were still enough fields for hay, and some room for the herd to graze. Nevertheless cows still roamed all over the property including the three campuses of the Seniors, Intermediates, and Juniors.

Part of Alex Grant's plan in having gardens and animals was to expose city boys to rural life, and to challenge them with hard farm work as part of their education for life. Alex Grant wanted more than food for the camp. In those days he had no problem in getting people to do farm chores and to care for the cows and other farm animals in addition to regular counselor duties. A number of camp jobs were done by boys in the fifteen-to-eighteen-year-old age bracket selected from the seniors or junior counselors. For many it was an honor to be chosen for some of these chores. For doing this, a few received partial scholarships and others a free summer. Some counselors were expected to come up pre-season to open the camp and do painting and cleanup from the past winter. The hours were long but the camaraderie superb. Some of the young men learned to handle cows and milking, and others took charge of the vegetable gardens, or supervised the harvesting of corn in season.

Woozie Supplee and Carlos Cardeza handled some of the dairy work, ran the cream separator, and made ice cream. Woozie (Henderson Supplee, Jr.) in later life delivered milk with a horse and wagon for Supplee-Wills-Jones Milk Company and eventually became president, then changed jobs leading to Chairman of Atlantic Refining Company in 1964. He had a lifetime commitment to Camp Tecumseh and was one of the original Trustees selected by Alex Grant. The nickname Woozie stuck during his whole life, a name given him by his little sister who, putting her fingers through his boyhood hair, said, "This feels Woozie."

A Successful Blend

In the 1920s before electricity came to Tecumseh a hand-cranked centrifugal separator produced cream for the ice cream served daily.

Camp Tecumseh

The girls of Singing Eagle Lodge often came to Tecumseh for dances. Camp director Doc Gibson is in the center of this 1920s photo.

On the fourteen-mile trip up Mt. Lafayette and down through the Flume in 1920

45

Occasionally the entire camp would be called out to do some weeding. Volunteers were also sought to harvest corn. Then there were some hourly jobs for the Junior boys who wanted spending money. They snapped string beans for the kitchen.

Because one of Mr. Grant's favorite foods was sweet corn, large fields were planted in the spring. In early August the first corn would be ready, and Mr. Grant's corn lecture would be given. "Corn when harvested has its maximum sugar content. It immediately starts conversion from sugar to starch and therefore must be cooked as soon as possible after picking, and then served right away."

The system called for the picking crew to go to the fields one-half hour before a meal, and then deliver the corn to the kitchen when the dinner bell rang. In a few minutes the corn would be steamed and served. Mr. Grant always claimed that there were no health problems after corn season had begun and as the season progressed there were times when corn would be on the table at *every* meal. Those who had the Tecumseh experience can never be satisfied with grocery counter corn.

By 1921 the Hollingsworth Farm was fully used by Tecumseh. Fred J. Doolittle and his wife Harriet

Williams Doolittle joined the staff and moved into the farmhouse on the second floor. Granny Williams, then in her nineties, came with them. The Sub-Juniors slept on the porches with Carlos Cardeza and Woozie Supplee as counselors. They had the advantage of screened porches whereas all the other campuses were pestered by mosquitoes, especially during June. They had meals with the rest of the camp in the dining hall. Mrs. Doolittle was the "house mother," and she also looked after

A Successful Blend

Camp Tecumseh, Moultonboro, on L

Fred J. Doolittle, grass cutter, counselor, and later teacher, in 1922. He became Associate Director of the camp in 1924.

Phyllis and Eenie who could not stay at the Point House alone. Since Fred Doolittle taught Latin and Greek at the Episcopal Academy, he was known to many boys from that school and had become a good friend of Alex Grant. He was famous for his slow manner of speaking and for his great interest in forestry and tree planting.

With only a nine-week camp season, it was essential to have a good farmer living on the property. Fod Boody, the farmer prior to 1919 had left to work at Geneva Point. One of the best men to come along was F. Clinton Grace who in 1921 was thirty-one years old. Assistants over the years included George Hathaway who had his own small farm down the road, and a helper, Horace Fife, who ate his meals in the kitchen and was quite a philosopher when you got him talking. These men had the camp and the Tecumseh farm to tend all year, a dairy herd with cows to milk, hay to grow

epesaukee, N.H. ...... July 12. 1922.

Photo by
P. Arakelyan
Harvard Sq. Studio
Camb. Mass.

and harvest, and extensive grounds and buildings to care for. Clint and his wife lived in the farmhouse except during the summers when they moved into a small cottage that Clint had built near the barn which Clint called "The Breeding Pen." Gordon Yocum recalls that Clint was something of a kidder, a salty talker and had a never-ending stream of jokes. He used to say, "I can fix it or I can fix it so nobody else can fix it."

After season there was lots of work to do in addition to the usual closing chores. The first few days were spent taking down tents, cleaning and storing the boats, and securing the engine house and the ice cream apparatus as well as other battening down activities prior to winter.

Phyllis Grant remembered,

Then on to the gardens always loaded with green beans, tomatoes, and corn. The counselors who stayed over did the picking, and my sister Eenie and I washed the beans, shucked the corn and stemmed the tomatoes. Lucy Johnson, as head cook, did the actual canning. I have no idea of the number of quart and gallon jars but it seemed like a hundred. A sizable working crew snapped the beans, cut the corn off the cob, and skinned the tomatoes.

It was always a race to get everything at least picked before the equinox set in. After the rain started, we didn't mind the time spent in the kitchen. Camp in the rain with no campers around is pretty dreary.

The canned goods were stored for use the following year before the garden crops came in.

The Tecumseh Cows

Bill Lingelbach, Jr. still remembers the day of his first arrival following the long train and boat ride, and then being assigned a cot on a tent platform in the woods with seven other boys. During the night he awoke to the nudge of a huge cow hovering

48

Counselor Henderson (Wooz) Supplee, Jr. (center) and his tentmates in 1922. A close friend of Alex Grant, he was one of the several original trustees named by Grant to ensure continuation of the camp from 1946 on.

over his face with her head in the tent. Bill wished he were back home!

Most city boys had never been exposed to a farm, and they soon learned lots of lessons never to be seen in regular school life. With Tecumseh Pontiac as a registered bull, others with cows on

Moultonboro Neck would bring them over one at a time to be bred, and the word would get around to come and watch this activity. Ed Stanley remembers that "one day *two* cows were paraded through the main campus en route to the breeding area and the cry of 'double-header at the farmhouse' rang throughout the camp." Better than any biology or sex-education class!

During the 1920s Bill Lingelbach, Jr. took charge of the cows and the milking with Todd Fritz assisting. Todd became an expert milker and set a record for milking three cows in a row without rest—a feat few could equal.

The farmer at that time was a man named Clark who was always chewing tobacco. Flies were annoying and Clark used to see a fly on the wall while he was milking. Said he, "See that fly over they-ah! Watch me drown 'im!" And a well-placed shot of tobacco juice would smother the fly!

One Sunday a cow was being led up the hill past the Lodge to another field with the rope halter securely wrapped around Mr. Grant's wrist. The cow began to run, Mr. Grant slipped, and was being dragged along the hillside with all the boys watching from the porch. There were numerous cow flops on the field, and the boys yelled, "Look out! Heads up! Here comes another one!" This was the end of Mr. Grant's white shirt and knickers. (It was a long-standing custom to wear white on Sundays.)

The Lingelbachs

William E. Lingelbach, Bill's father, was about five years older than Alex Grant, and Grant always looked up to him as an older friend. They started their friendship at the University of Toronto where Bill, Sr. was in the class of 1896. Later he became Chairman of the Department of History at the University of Pennsylvania. Alex Grant's B.A. degree was in history.

Bill, Jr. became the head counselor of the Senior Campus in 1926. He was a Rhodes Scholar at Oxford from 1926 to 1929, then taught at Penn Charter for awhile. Later he went into law as a career. He has continued his active association with

Tecumseh ever since and was one of the founding trustees named by Alex Grant's will to take over management of the camp in 1946,

Mary and Lucy, the Cooks

The key to good food at Tecumseh has always been the wonderfully capable cooks. Phyllis never forgot Mary.

Back in the early 20s we had a West Indian chef—Jim Rogers—a very handsome man and capable cook. The pastry cook was a black woman, Mary. I never knew her last name. Her pies and cakes were delicious but as time went on during the season, her need for vanilla began to become unreasonable. With a little checking the reason turned out to be it was her "comfort" in the long dull evenings before bed time. I think they provided her with the amount she "needed" for the rest of the summer but she wasn't rehired. I can empathize with her: with no books, no magazines or radio, nor any other woman to talk to, life would be pretty rough!

When the kitchen floor was replaced by Buster McCormack some years later, a pile of old vanilla bottles was found from Mary's day.

Then there were the famous cinnamon buns started by Lucy Johnson in the 20s. Phyllis' memory is good.

Anyone who has ever tasted this nectar of the gods will never find an equal. Sunday night supper for many years was composed of cold sliced pork sandwiches, platters of sliced tomtoes, ice-cold milk and cinnamon buns. I can see Lucy Johnson early Sunday afternoon rolling out sheets of dough, lathering them with real butter, drifting brown sugar over them, studding them with raisins and cinnamon. [Lew Tabor siad that one of the secrets of these was the use of grape sugar which made an excellent soft sugar syrup coating.] This done, she'd roll up the dough and cut it into slices and set the buns on huge baking pans for the final rising. When the sandwich crew came in to start supper preparations, the buns would go into the ovens. Half an hour or so later they were turned out, cooled, and put on huge platters for the tables. These were huge buns—about 4 inches thick and running over with delicious goo.

Doc Orton Leaves

In the early 1920s, with Doc Orton continuing also to run his Camp Iroquois, the relationship between him and Alex Grant steadily worsened. On June 14, 1924, Orton and his wife signed a deed conveying their share of Tecumseh to Grant, thus finally ending the old partnership.

50

Introducing Henry Williams

In addition to Walter Johnson, another dramatist began his long tenure with Camp Tecumseh in 1921. Henry Williams, an extraordinary fellow with a keen sense of humor, was a good writer and made a career of teaching drama at Dartmouth College. Henry was fourteen when he first came to Tecumseh. He graduated from Penn Charter in 1924, next studied art, and then went on to Yale for a Master of Fine Arts degree. During summers he was a counselor at Tecumseh. One of his earliest contributions was the founding of a weekly camp newspaper in 1929. Volume I, No. 1 has survived; it has two pages. Said Henry Williams, "When someone approached for a title . . . like the dawn breaking over the 'Three Sisters' . . . came the little gem 'The Tecumseh Sunbeam' and the masthead motto: 'It's the light that burns and not the heat. —A. Grant.' "

The golf team in 1929. Standing are Dave McMullin, Lewis Tabor, Bill Weaver, and Ralph Johnson. In front are Bob McKee, Bill Scheetz, and Bill Barnes.

Morning Exercise at Camp Tecumseh 1923

51

Henry Williams joined the Dartmouth faculty in 1931 in the English Department and became full professor in 1950. His efforts in theater there won him much acclaim and he finally had the title of Professor Emeritus at his death on November 26, 1987. He was back at Tecumseh most summers to help direct Gilbert and Sullivan productions of which he was an authority on set and costume design.

Walter Johnson as a writer and director put on some hilarious skits and musicals. One of Walter's dramas was a "Novelty Minstrel Act" title *OH! MAN!* which had as its setting the days when the Lodge was "occupied by a combined poor house and insane asylum. It is the purpose of this play to take you back to those days. . . . It is a composite result of swiping plot, words, and music from everything available and serves to point out that there is not so much difference between an insane asylum and a boy's camp after all."

Tecumseh Day, 1920

For Tecumseh Day, 1920, the last event of every season when parents were invited, the following history was written.

When old Sol rose over the silvery lake and poured its golden rays over Tecumseh it was surprised to see many stirring. . . . Walter Johnson and the company had a rehearsal. . . . Then a swim, and after that Tecumseh punch (mixed graped juice and orange juice), cake, ice cream, and salad surely tasted fine. . . . Then the usual Hill-Tecumseh ball game. We found to our distress that the Wolfeboro team was more than our match for we were defeated 17-2. Nevertheless we enjoyed the game very much. . . . We all went down to the beach for a swim in our bathing suits (. . . useless luxuries). We had a light supper. Last the big event of the day was staged . . . a musical comedy called Jack Roses *written by Walter Johnson . . . staged in the dining hall, a curtain with an Indian Head painted by Dr. O'Brien upon it adorned the front of the stage. A record crowd was stuffed into the Hall.*

A Successful Blend

52

The historian of the day added:

And when the show was over, Tecumseh Day was past
The moon was in the Western sky, The bonfire glowed its last.
All praise is due to Walter, And to his faithful crew,
Of real devoted campers, Who put the big show through.

A letter of May 22, 1921, to Walter Johnson just before he left on an extended overseas journey, shows Mr. Grant's admiration.

I can't begin to tell you how much we are going to miss you at Camp. Walter, no one has ever meant more. You have given some of your best years and when the boys speak of you, and they speak true, they don't center on your playing—wonderful as that was—nor on your many other activities, but they speak of what you are yourself. That is what the camp is and all that it is as I know it.

I will try to make myself feel that the camp is so much bigger than anything we are that I must be indifferent to my personal feelings in putting forward what I know to be right so that when you come back you may find the best of what you left still flourishing. There have been many wonderful boys and men. Very sincerely yours, Alex Grant.

Jottings

Doc Orton's Amazing Run

Mountain trips had changed a little with the addition of a Ford Model T truck to haul the blanket rolls and food instead of the horse and wagon. Doc Orton excelled in mountain climbing and before withdrawing from Tecumseh set a record for running up Mt. Washington. He checked his watch, ran up and checked in at the Tip Top House where he informed the manager that he had just set a record. The man refused to believe him since he hadn't checked in at the base, so Doc Orton told him, "I'll run down and do it over again!" The story concludes that he did just that all in the same day!

Additions to the Staff

In 1924 Fred J. Doolittle became associate director and Forrest L. Gager joined the Council. Some others who came in the 1920s and who maintained a long relationship with the camp as counselors and/or Trustees included David McMullin III in 1920; Henry B. Williams and William G. Hamilton, Jr. in 1921; William H. Harman, Jr. and Lewis P. Tabor in 1923; H. Hayes Aikens and Drew Pearsall in 1924; Alvin S. Wagner, William H. Ortlepp, and Arthur Chase in 1925; Edward L. Stanley and Joseph W. Carnwath in 1926; Bertram P. Shover and Herbert Munger in 1927; William F. Tiernan, Jr. in 1928; and George Stanley in 1929.

In addition, already in active roles from the 1909-1919 period, were Henderson Supplee, Jr. (Woozie), Wallace Arnold, Bill Lingelbach, Jr., Ralph Johnson, Walter Johnson, and David C. Spooner, Jr. With this pool of loyal leadership under Mr. Grant's direction, the best years of camp were still to come.

5

Drama and Great Pianists

1930 – 1939

A GROWING DEPRESSION which began in this decade made it difficult to recruit boys and maintain a full program. The tuition had been $350 for nine weeks for several years, but Mr. Grant lowered it to $300 in 1933 where it remained for at least ten years. Although there were some improvements made in camp facilities, the kitchen stoves still burned wood, refrigeration depended upon ice cut from the lake, and water was still pumped by a gasoline engine at the lakefront. Because of his dedication Mr. Grant drew on the cash value of his life insurance to keep the camp afloat.

Gilbert and Sullivan Tradition Begins

Henry Williams really made this a decade of drama. When he started teaching at Dartmouth in 1931 and further developed his theater interests there, he also brought Gilbert and Sullivan to Tecumseh, a tradition that has continued ever since. Henry, in his research on theatrical costumes of various periods, was also a costume designer and set designer as well as a writer and director. Producing a new play just about every week required a vivid imagination and lots of cooperation and hard work.

When Walter Johnson returned from Europe, he started an interior decorating business at 526 Madison Avenue in New York City which he ran from 1924 to 1942. However, whenever he could get some time off he would appear at camp and assist Henry Williams as a pianist and drama coach. Walter enjoyed his hobby of music so much that he changed careers after World War II and went to Westminster Choir College in Princeton where he taught until he retired in 1963 at seventy years of age. This gave him more time to be at Tecumseh and share his talents with many boys. He had a

---

World Events of the Decade

1930	Naval disarmament treaty signed.	1935	Social Security Act passed.
1931	*Star Spangled Banner* becomes national anthem.	1936	Chiang Kai-shek declares war on Japan.
1932	Nylon invented.	1937	Lincoln Tunnel opens.
1933	Japan withdraws from League of Nations.	1938	Devastating hurricane hits New England.
1934	*S.S. Queen Mary* launched.	1939	Germany invades Poland.

Lovely maidens from a Gilbert and Sullivan operetta in the 1930s

54

Henry Williams at his intermediates' tent, circa 1934. Professor of dramatics at Dartmouth for 41 years, a lover of Gilbert and Sullivan and one of Tecumseh's greatest humorists and historians. "He has touched us all with his magic and we shall never forget him."

Camp Tecumseh

Bill Watkins, musical director of the first Gilbert and Sullivan produced in 1931

Joe Lorraine and his banjo return, "completing 55 years of entertaining in the Winnepesaukee region."

Eugene List, camp pianist, at the age of sixteen. His later world concerts included a performance at Potsdam in 1945 before Truman, Churchill, and Stalin.

favorite expression in speaking to a boy: "You CAN do it!"

Very late in life he tried to learn to drive—sometimes with disastrous results—but he was never hurt in an accident. He would climb from the ditch or his overturned car saying, "Now I've done it!" and then he would ask a friend to find him another used car and start over again. His life was totally absorbed in the arts.

Almost every year *Cox and Box*, a short one-act farce, would start the dramatic season at camp. Brooks Keffer, Richard Ryan and Ralph Johnson were the actors for many years. Then came the original skits with a collection of characters unheard of on any other stage, names like Diana Dishwater (played by Bob Eckles) and the lecherous Rizpuddin (played by Dik Pakradooni). The serial thrillers which ran for several weeks were introduced and mostly written by Henry Williams. Typical was one in 1935 entitled *The Love Life and Adventures of Esmeralda* or *The Mad Monster's Monstrous Mistake* with the cast of:

Abijah Rattletrap	Dick Seymer
Lucille Rattletrap	George Stanley
Abner Shadfish	B. Herman Jarman ("Pop")
Miguel Catalepsy	C.H. Snyder
Esmeralda Pushcan	Jack Havens
Frankenfurter	Robert Eckles
Loring Q. Goodheart	H. Aikens

Joe Lorraine Returns

A variation for entertainment was the arrival of comedian-storyteller-bell ringer Joe Lorraine who started his one-man show in 1899. He returned to camp in 1933 and came regularly until 1949. The *Sunbeam* reported,

Also returned were Joe's famed cow-bells and banjo. But the banjo he played for a cheering Tecumsaudience last Monday night was not the one with which Joe had entertained thousands for many years and which he had strummed to A.E.F. doughboys in over 650 concerts at the "front." Joe confided "I haven't got the old one any

Alex Grant and Jiller girl, a gift from the council, in 1934

56

Alex Grant with Bo-Bo, the scottie whose tussles with Jiller the husky were legendary

Bertram (Pinky) Shover in 1939. Teacher at Episcopal and later Grosse Pointe Country Day, he ran the Tecumseh tutoring program

more. That was a historic instrument—the most famous banjo in the world. I think the government put it in a museum—the Smithsonian, they call it."

Following his Dr. Holmes thriller, yarnspinner Lorraine lightened the fare, spun his famed anecdotes. . . . What Tecumsmen awaited most eagerly, however, were Joe Lorraine's famed imitations. Said he: "Note how close these come to perfection." Saws, trains, mosquitoes, grinding wheels, all these were easy for facile-mouthed Joe. "Most difficult imitation ever give" was the auto race. . . . Said he, "I was afraid I'd never get that race over . . . too much soup for supper." Tecumsmen wanted "Dracula" but to no avail. Said Joe: "No Dracula tonight, boys. It's too powuhful!"

Perhaps words like *Tecumsmen* need explanation. Henry Williams introduced all sorts of words like this into The *Sunbeam* weekly news whenever he wanted to use Camp Tecumseh as a modifier. He would use *Tecums* followed by any noun, place, or person; e.g., *Tecumsdock*, *Tecumsfixit*, *Tecumsdrama*, *Tecumsites*, and more.

Some Famous Pianists at Tecumseh

Piano music was another highlight on the *Tecumscene*. Mr. Grant always tried to have an accomplished pianist at camp. Some mentioned in the 1930s include Terranova, Walter Johnson, Dr. Tongue, Walter Chudnowsky, Waldemar Dabrowski, Robert Eckles and two exceptionally talented young men-Eugene List and Willy Kapell. Walter Chudnowsky was a counselor from 1931 to 1933 and *Sunbeam* editor who then went to England as a Rhodes Scholar for three years culminating in his winning the President's Prize at Balliol College.

Continuing the traditions of good music of the earlier years, Alex Grant was able to establish some superb friendly relations with leaders in the music world including Madame Olga Samaroff, pianist, teacher at the Curtis Institute, and former wife of Leopold Stokowski, conductor of the Philadelphia Orchestra. Alex would ask her for promising young students of hers and offer them a free summer at Tecumseh.

Camp Tecumseh

Pyramid in 1933 includes (from top) Pinky Shover, Bob McDonald, Bub Toebe, Stu Brown, Ed Stanley, Bill Richards, Dik Pakradooni, Bill Tiernan, Hayes Aikens, and Joe Carnwath.

Drama and Great Pianists

Clint Grace clears the way at the farm with a snow scoop during the winter of 1935

58

Haying in 1935. George Hathaway is on the load.

The senior baseball team of 1935. Standing are Craig Adair, George Stanley, Jack Havens, and Dick Christopher. Seated are Dick Havens, Rodney McDowell, and Horace Schwarz.

Camp Tecumseh

In the early 1930s she sent Eugene List (born in 1918) who made his debut at age twelve with the Los Angeles Philharmonic in New York on December 19, 1935, in the American premiere of Shostakovich's piano concerto. As a sergeant in the U.S. Army, he gained special recognition when he performed before Truman, Churchill, and Stalin at the Potsdam Conference in July 1945. Later President Truman frequently invited him to perform at the White House. He died suddenly in April 1984, at age 66, a few months before he was scheduled to play at Carnegie Hall to celebrate the fiftieth anniversary of his debut there.

List was followed by Willy Kapell (born in 1922) during the 1938-1941 period. Most boys shy away from classical piano, but Willy, practicing two to three hours per day in the dining room, drew boys and staff of all ages to watch, listen, and find a new perspective on music they otherwise would have missed. Willy was friendly and fit in well. He loved

Heavy snow at the Junior A Pagoda in 1935

60

Waiting for the train at Meredith in 1937. "Stand back of the yellow line!"

to play and no one wanted him to stop. Grant told Doc Ann Gibson at Singing Eagle Lodge about the young pianist and loaned Willy for an evening. The girls loved his playing. "My most vivid memory . . . was the playing of Willy Kapell, late into the night until Mr. George suggested driving him back to Tecumseh," said Singing Eagle's Carol Johnstone Sharp forty years later.

As waterfront director and *Tecumscounselor* from 1938 to 1940, Steve Hammond remembered teaching Willy Kapell to swim and listening to him play the piano. "He was a superb pianist and finally he did learn to swim. It wasn't easy, but I managed!" Baseball was a forbidden sport since Willy had to avoid any possibility of injury to his hands.

When he turned twenty-five, a newspaper article stated,

Perhaps the most significant thing about Willy Kapell beside the fact that at age twenty-five he ranks among the world's great pianists, is his unassuming friendliness. . . . He manages a modesty and simple mode of living not always associated with youthful success.

Occasionally Mr. Grant would invite some parents to have Sunday dinner with him in the dining hall. At dessert time he would ask his guests whether they would like to hear one of the boys play the piano. Politely they agreed.

Mr. Grant would rise and motion with his typical outstretched hand, "Willy, could you play something for our guests?" And the young lad would amaze and astound everyone with a Chopin Polonaise from memory on the old upright piano.

Then tragedy struck on October 29, 1953, when thirty-one-year-old Willy, returning from an Australian concert tour, died in an airplane crash two minutes before a scheduled landing in San Francisco in a fog.

Eugene Istomin (born in 1925), a protege of Rudolph Serkin, was a promising young pianist who spent a portion of the 1941 season at camp when he was sixteen. Istomin went on to become another highly successful pianist who continues on

Lucy Johnson, queen of the kitchen, in 1937

Floree, Lucy Johnson's daughter, was queen of the laundry during the same era.

A week's laundry spanking clean and ready for pickup on a Sunday morning in 1938

Jim Birney paints his name on the Lodge wall in 1937, a custom dating from the earliest days

the concert tour circuit in 1992. In 1975 he married Martitia Casals, widow of Pablo Casals, the composer–cellist.

In the late 1940s the visiting pianist was George Reeves who shared his talents for several summers.

Drama and Great Pianists

62

Junior B's baseball on a fine summer afternoon in 1937

Camp Tecumseh

The 1938 Junior B fire, a spectacular blaze

The 1938 Junior B fire continued a long tradition. Firemakers Bud Toebe and Bob McDonald flank the juniors.

Drama and Great Pianists

64

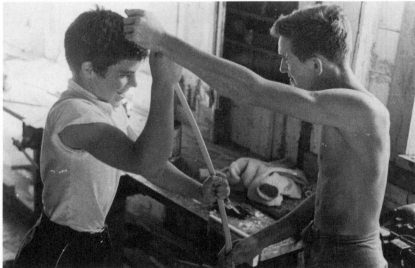

Ely tries the bend of the lemonwood bow he's making in the shop in 1939

Camp Tecumseh

A great quartet of friends. Walter Johnson, Alex Grant, Jiller, and Arthur Armstrong who became the first president of the board of trustees after Grant's death in 1946

65

An Alumni Reunion

In 1930 five Tecumseh alumni—James Gould, Harry M. (Pushface) Jones, Alfred D. Norris, David C. Spooner, Jr., and Joseph K. T. Van Pelt—had a reunion at camp that summer and lived together in a tent by the lake. They had a marvelous vacation—"men of divers viewpoints, ages, and modes of living."

At the end of their vacation they wrote:

We have felt the atmosphere of enthusiasm and youth, of which we were once a part. We realize now that the days at Camp were the happiest we knew, and possibly the most helpful in forming our characters along those lines which make for success and happiness; sportsmanship; courage in competition; social responsibility; service. Needless to say, we know that a large proportion of the health and energy we enjoy today, we owe to Camp Tecumseh.

Sunday bath day for modest Nelson Degerberg and Roy Miller in 1939

Drama and Great Pianists

Forrest Gager, The Red Fox

"Did the Red Fox catch you?" was a familiar theme around camp in the 1930s. Forrest Gager was known by this nickname for many years because of his uncanny appearance at the wrong time when some antics had been going on. A typical situation was reported in the *Sunbeam* in 1935:

"Another famous *Tecumsbaseball* man was discovered beyond escape when he made the mistake of not returning to Camp until 4 o'clock of one brilliant sunrise, meeting Mr. Gager just as the latter was starting out on a day's work."

How the name Red Fox originated is unknown, although his red hair and the way he bounded about the camp property made it a most appropriate one. Bus Gager (his son) shared one incident. "One pre-season Dick Whitney arrived during a meal. Bert Shover was at the head of the table and as Dick came in the corner door, he said: 'Hi, Bert, where's the Fox?' 'Right here,' was heard from one of the side chairs along the wall. For once, Dick was speechless!"

Forrest Lee Gager was born July 29, 1895, grew up on a dairy farm, attended a one-room school in Cold Spring, Pennsylvania, then went on to graduate from West Chester State Normal School in 1913. He had the amazing record of teaching school for fifty-five years, mostly at the Episcopal Academy, then a few years at the Booth School, and never missed a day because of sickness! His association with Camp Tecumseh began about 1924 and continued into the 1970s. He was a part owner of the camp and acted as treasurer and bookkeeper for many years. In 1939 he was listed as associate director in the annual camp brochure for the first time.

Henry Williams called the mechanically minded men of the staff *Technocrats*, in which he included Gager, Lewis Tabor, Ralph Johnson, and later Charlie Hargens and Fred Clark. He also referred to *Tecumsfixit* Gager. Others called Mr. Gager *Gage*, and he had many daily chores including running the pump house and the chlorinator at the lakefront.

Gage had an office in the Trunk Room and spent long hours during the nights and early mornings keeping the books, paying the help, filing taxes and all the paperwork to keep the business side in order. He and farmer Clint Grace worked well together. He also had a reputation for record-breaking speed driving to Center Harbor for the evening mail, and for blueberry picking expeditions to Mt. Major in the 1927 Packard touring car.

Jim Wenck took a job one summer at camp with certain assigned chores.

I had a big run-in with Forrest Gager one summer. . . . I got some job I didn't feel like doing and I refused to do it. . . . The Red Fox picked me up by the scruff of the neck. . . . I was fourteen years old and I weighed 170 pounds. He said, "Jim, you as a man made a contract to come up here and work and do certain tasks, and we as men made a contract with you that we would give you your summer in return for you doing certain tasks. Now, if you violate your contract we're going to put you on a train and send you home." I got the message! It was a marvellous lesson.

Transformation of the Trunk Room

In 1933 portions of the Trunk Room got a transformation, as reported in the *Sunbeam*:

Peacefully sitting in the Sunbeam *office Williams and Ye Ed. were suddenly startled . . . by a banging at the door and a voice that sounded very much like that of Tecumseh's Mr. Gager. "Open the door or we'll break it in!" We discovered standing at the door, holding a varied assortment of menacing massive jimmies and crow-bars, those famous technicians Messrs. Gager, Johnson, and Tabor, arrayed in the latest style togs for a wrecking expedition.*

"Sock it to 'er," proclaimed head-wrecker Gager, whereupon amid the most horrific din, dust, and clamor, the old order yielded, the manual training shop was completely denuded of its battle scarred benches, the Sunbeam *office was rent in twain, the Drama retreated to its closet.*

Out of the project came a new room for tutoring and rehearsals, a *Sunbeam* office, a drama office, a manual training area, and a writing room. With a

Forrest L. Gager, known as "the Fox," in 1938; a loyal friend of Alex Grant, teacher at Episcopal for fifty-five years, an associate director, and a true "Mr. Fixit."

Camp Tecumseh

The Trunk Room in 1939. The study and tutoring room where Pinky Shover ruled was on the front floor left; Gager's office was to the right of the open barn door.

The gardens and the new widow in 1936

new spray gun everything was painted ivory, getting rid of the aluminum of the past. The tutoring room was to be equipped with a transcription of Shover's voice with a selection to be made by pushing buttons which would give a choice of messages: 1. "Come out of the daze; you're paying good money for this tutoring." 2. "Well, if you want to, we can stay here all night!" 3. "Stop reading those jokes and concentrate on this spelling!"

In typical *Sunbeam* style the article on the new facilities concluded: "The Drama and the *Sunbeam* invite you all to *Tecumup* and *Tecumsee* us sometime!"

End of the "Widow"

Newcomers at camp were left wondering when someone said, "I'm off to the widow." Oldtimers knew the *widow* (sometimes spelled "widdow") to be the toilet facility but no one could explain why or who first named it. For over thirty years the *widow* was a dug trench and the usual wooden seats in what most call a privy or outhouse. There were small ones near each campus. Then in 1935 skilled farmer Clint Grace built a new building with ten flush toilets, screened sides, and a lavatory—a startling bit of modernization! The end of the privy was celebrated at the annual Junior B fire. According to the *Sunbeam*

Counselors Ehmke, Stanley, and McCracken erected a pyre of logs, remnants of the beach stage and branches. This year's innovation was the, Jr. B widow blandly perched on top of the burning WHOLE. The Jr. B's labeled the edifice: "THE FLUSH TOOK MY FULL HOUSE." The fire blazed merrily, warmed even the dampest.

The *Thetis*

One of Forrest Gager's pet projects was the *Thetis*, an old wooden lake boat he reportedly rescued from years of sitting on the bottom somewhere, and in which he installed a Star automobile 4-cylinder engine, the reliability of which was forever in question. The *Sunbeam* description by Aram Pakradooni tells more:

To A Sea Nymph
The Thetis *is a motor boat,*
That has an awful time to float.
Years ago it had a top.
But now it's just an awful flop.

When they pulled it from the lake,
With many a groan and grunt and ache.
They didn't realize what trouble
Was coming up with every bubble.

Ralph Cornelius Johnson in 1938. A teacher at Hill School and shepherd to the intermediates for many years who became director of Hill Camp in the mid-1950s

Drama and Great Pianists

The refurbished Thetis *on the bottom in 1938 because the captain forgot to shut a valve*

Chief gardener Alex Grant in the tomato patch in 1930

After a year of patient work,
The new one started with a jerk,
Across the lake they really tore
But they came back by means of oar.

Neophytes Clark and Hargens took over in 1937 and put the *Thetis* in first class (?) order. They took off, and chagrined were these engineers when ten minutes later the *Thetis* was paddled back to its position at the dock. Said Gager, "Things are running as usual this season."

By the end of August the boat was seaworthy and trustworthy enough for Mr. Grant to approve a trip to the broads for 25 Junior B's with licensed Master, Pilot, and Engineer Clark at the helm. All went well until on the way home Captain Clark gave the wheel to one of the boys. Then Clark buried himself in the script for the evening melodrama. Suddenly there was a great jolt and the *Thetis* came to rest in the middle of what is now shown on the charts as "The Graveyard," at that time unmarked by buoys. The *Thetis* was freed after all the boys lined up on one side of the boat and at a signal jumped together to the other side. Very slowly the *Thetis* was maneuvered out of the Graveyard and purred (?) back to camp after dinner had already begun.

The author and captain of the Thetis *on top of Mt. Lafayette in 1937*

Agriculture At Its Zenith

The farm and gardens at Tecumseh probably reached their zenith in the 1930s. In 1931, 20,000 ears of corn were picked for the camp tables, an all-time record. In addition to a dairy herd of 20 cows, there were 800 laying chickens, and another 1000 chickens for eating. Pork completed the meat variety.

The head gardener and his main assistant were counselors and this was practically a full assignment for which they earned their board and a small salary. Art Armstrong (later a Trustee) came as head gardener. Bill Decker for example was offered $50 for the season in the mid-1930s. Boys were given the chance to work by the hour. Bill Scheetz's notebook titled "Agriculture 1932" showed earnings of 20 cents per hour by Elkins Wetherill, C. Adair, N. Degerberg, and Fernald while younger boys earned 15 cents per hour, including T. McDonald, C. Wetherill, C. Hires, S. McCracken, R. Havens, and J. Heppe. High pay of 25 cents went to Benton, P. Salom, and Anderson.

Following Decker came Lee Bird and Gordon Yocum with Fred Bird as assistant. Gordon Yocum recalled the appropriate verse:

Their hearts completely hardening,
They gave their minds to gardening
For raising beans was something they adored!

Camp Tecumseh

One of the several garden patches in 1939 which made the camp self-sufficient in vegetables

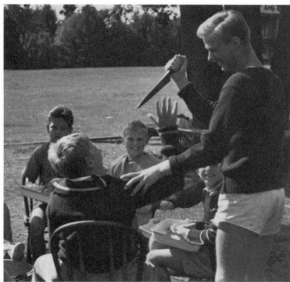

Gardener Lee Bird urging faster bean snapping from his crew in 1936. Wages ranged from 15 to 25 cents an hour.

Alex Grant's beloved flower garden in 1937; source of sweet pea bouquets for visiting ladies

Drama and Great Pianists

70

Ed Stanley Remembers

Facts and history are unimportant when compared with the results of the Tecumseh experience. So we close the 1930s with this memory of Ed Stanley (Tecumseh 1926 to 1936), Episcopal and Williams College graduate, and currently a Trustee of Camp Tecumseh:

I loved everything about my eleven years at camp—the beauty of the place, the daily life, the sports, the men who ran it, my fellow campers and the friendships we formed. Alex Grant became almost a second father to me, both because of the things he stood for and because of the interest he took in my personal development. . . . I wanted to live up to his own standards. . . . My favorite memory is of his conducting our evening prayer service in the Lodge before going off to bed . . . and the words he often spoke: "We thank thee Lord for our life here in your great out-of-doors." No religious services before or since have moved me as much.

#1123 shows her stuff on Winnipesaukee the same year

Jottings

The New Chris-Craft

A notable addition for 1935 was a new Chris-Craft which Ralph Johnson thereafter drove back annually from Lakeport and its winter storage. On Sundays during swim hour at noon Mr. Grant enjoyed driving the boat used for aquaplaning, and frequently lost track of time, irritating Mrs. Lucy Johnson who had dinner ready at one o'clock sharp. Although water skiing had been pioneered in France in 1920, it didn't come to Tecumseh until 1953.

Nighttime Adventure

A tremendous explosion at 4:00 A.M. one August morning in 1937 woke most Tecumsites. Said Al Wagner, "They're only dynamiting the road early to avoid traffic. Go back to bed, all of you!" On the Senior Campus many of us jumped up and pajama-clad ran to the beach where across the lake we could see the flames of the Elkins Boathouse. Excited and ready for an adventure, a number of us piled into two war canoes and took off across the lake to see the fire, and the Tecumseh motorboat with ten on board roared over also. There was nothing we could do except pick up floating debris and deposit it on shore, and observe the charred remains of several speedboats, their steering wheels being the only portion spared by the fire. The explosion was the dynamiting of the dock to keep the fire from spreading to the house by the shore. Through all this, Forrest Gager slept!

The Hurricane of 1938

The hurricane of 1938 was one of the worst ever to hit New Hampshire, and Camp Tecumseh lost a huge number of trees which a local sawmill made into lumber for future projects. By good fortune it occurred in late September when no one was at camp except Josiah McCracken, Jr. and his new bride on their honeymoon, staying at the Point Cottage. There was a privy out back which was demolished by a fallen tree but the honeymooners were unharmed, a memory never forgot-

Camp alumnus Edward L. Davis presented the Boston and Maine locomotive bell shown here atop the dining hall in 1906 "In appreciation of all the good food at Tecumseh . . . ring this bell and no one will miss a meal."

ten. Mountain trips in 1939 were curtailed since large portions of the White Mountain Forest were closed because of the blowdowns and the fire danger.

Drama and Great Pianists

72

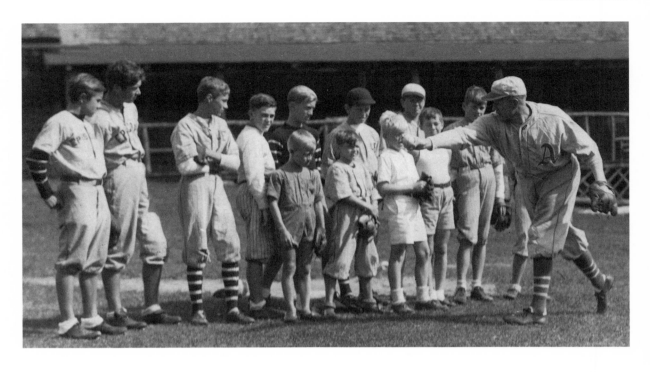

Howard Ehmke's Return

Famed baseball pitcher Howard Ehmke thrilled Tecumseh boys in the early 1930s when he returned and gave pointers to potential pitchers including Jack Havens, Ed Stanley, and Mason Fernald. Howard John Ehmke, born in 1894, was at camp in 1912 where he was already making records at age 18. On July 10 the *History* reported: "An unexpected game was played against Passa-wanaka . . . Tecumseh won 6-0, Howard Ehmke pitching a no-hit game." After serving with the Detroit Tigers from 1916-1922, the Boston Red Sox from 1923-1926, he joined the Philadelphia Athletics where Connie Mack surprised everyone by starting Ehmke in the first game of the World Series of 1929. Ehmke won the game, setting a new World Series record by striking out thirteen batters. The A's won the series. Howard died March 17, 1959, at age sixty-four.

6

A Time For Change

1940–1949

A TURNING POINT in Tecumseh history was to come in the decade of the 1940s. A normal start, then the World War II years, rationing of supplies, the death of Mr. Grant, and the challenge of seeking new leadership tested the traditions and goals of Tecumseh. Increasing costs and a debt burden cut the season from nine weeks to eight in 1946, and tuition rose to $400 in 1948. Seven Trustees began setting direction for the camp under Mr. Grant's will with Henderson Supplee, Jr. as chairman in 1946. All were long-time alumni of Camp Tecumseh and loyal to the ideals of Mr. Grant.

In 1940 the state imposed a requirement on the farm that milk must be pasteurized. To meet the new standards, a stainless steel pasteurizer was installed in the spring of 1940, and Mr. Grant asked engineering student Clark if he could install a 100 psi steam boiler ("psi" is pounds per square inch).

Larry Cloud (Junior Tecumseh Boy 1937) and Fred Clark built the chimney, which is still standing at the back of the kitchen, and did all the piping to hook up the steam boiler. On July 28th a roaring wood fire was built, the steam pressure held, and the sound of a steamboat issued from an antique whistle to celebrate successful completion of the project. Clark threw his duffle on the camp truck, said farewell, and was taken to Meredith station as he left for Union Carbide. After the cows were sold and pasteurizing ended, the boiler was used for many years to steam the sweet corn for the dining room.

Fred Clark Remembers

I first came to camp in June 1937 when at Lew Tabor's suggestion Mr. Grant had asked me to make charcoal for the kitchen stoves since I was a student of chemical engineering. Shortly after camp opened Mr. Grant called

---

World Events of the Decade

1940	Japan, Germany and Italy sign military pact.	1945	War in Europe ends May 8, in Japan August 14.
1941	Pearl Harbor, December 7.	1946	United Nations holds first meeting in London.
1942	Sugar, gasoline, and coffee rationing starts.	1947	Transistor invented by Bell Labs.
1943	Italy surrenders.	1948	Marshall Plan to rebuild Europe begins.
1944	"D" Day, June 6.	1949	Chaing Kai-Shek moves forces to Formosa.

73

Chimney built by Larry Cloud and the author in 1940 to serve the boiler for the dairy. The boiler was later converted to a corn cooker when the dairy was discontinued.

74

Charlie Shreiner soars toward the pit with Don Miller ready to measure

me in and explained that he had a crisis and needed help. The three boys from Boston who were the dishwashers were doing such a poor job that Lucy Johnson, the cook, refused to eat from any plate they washed, and kept her own plate locked up. That night without warning the three boys were awakened at 3:00 A.M., put on the camp truck, and delivered to the milk train which came through Meredith about 4:30 A.M. bound for Boston. "You'll be on the milk train" was clearly understood after that. My brother Charles and I washed dishes by hand for 150 persons after each meal the rest of the summer for which we were paid $50 each. At the seasons end I recommended to Mr. Grant that an electric dishwasher be purchased. The following June I arrived to find a Hobart dishwasher ready for me to install. In those days it was hand threading of galvanized pipe—great training for an engineer! Ever since then a dishwasher crew has been part of the kitchen chores for older boys. In 1948 "Beetle" Fiero together with John Roak, John Hancock, Reggie Wagner, and Bill Crockett were on that crew, while Pete Benoliel and Buddy Addis headed up the waiters.

Driving the Trucks

Driving the trucks was one aspect of camp life that several counselors aspired to each year. Charlie Hargens recalls Mr. Grant approaching him: "Charlie, what are your plans for the summer?" He wanted him at camp. "Of course there will be no remuneration!" he continued. Many were glad to get a job at Tecumseh and work long hours for the privilege of a healthy summer in a beautiful place.

On arrival at camp Mr. Gager got Charlie a New Hampshire "Chauffeur License" without examination at that time. Tecumseh had two main vehicles for transporting campers: an ancient 1927 Packard touring car, and a Ford V-8 stake body truck equipped with removable wooden benches. Standing up in the truck was found by most to be more comfortable than sitting on the springless benches, so for safety there was always a problem to make the boys sit during travel, especially on narrow mountain roads where tree limbs were low. Boys loved this kind of travel to mountain climbing areas. It is not permitted today.

Camp Tecumseh

Intermediates on the old basketball court in 1940

75

Truck drivers at Tecumseh learned quickly that the campers expected to stop on the way home for a "guzzle" at some store or soda fountain for treats. While ice cream was on the menu at camp almost every day, return from a hike was special and Hargens thought the boys liked to return to the urbanity from which they came by getting into a store.

About every other day one of the drivers made a trip to Center Harbor, Meredith, or Laconia for supplies. We would get orders from all over camp from boys and staff for some minor items wanted in addition to the list for the kitchen from the inimitable Lucy Johnson. It was very important to be on her side and to get *exactly* what she needed when she was out of something. No excuse was acceptable for returning to camp empty-handed. Sometimes you would be rewarded with a leftover cinnamon bun or a piece of cake she had hidden away.

As Hargens remembered, "We became very familiar with the camp supply houses in Laconia. At Palmer-Simpson's we would pull up to the loading dock in grand style and take on barrels . . . to feed the hungry camp. This was fun and we felt very important."

Truck drivers had some privileges including occasional access to "wheels" for personal evening use, i.e., dates, almost totally denied others for the season. "We were very careful not to abuse this. Mr. Grant always held out the penalty of shipping one out 'on the milk train' and the infrequent serious offender of camp rules really got this treatment." Over a period of years other truck drivers included Bill Tiernan, Ed Stanley, Don Miller, Pebble Stone, Bus Gager, Jim Fraser, Fred James, and Fred Clark.

World War II

With the advent of the war, followed by gasoline rationing, the 1942 season witnessed some major changes in camp life. Mountain trips, some athletic contests, and other journeys by automobile were curtailed. It also became obvious that transporting boys to camp in the family car would be impossible for their parents, so the train was the only solution.

Lewis P. Tabor in 1940. A quiet-spoken scientist from MIT, he taught at Episcopal, later became a consultant to Franklin Institute, and inspired many boys to go for a career in science or engineering.

A Time For Change

Rowing practice in 1942 with Morris, Osgood, Alvord,
Barnes, and Carradine maneuvering for position

A camper samples the splendor of Winnipesaukee from the
Ossipee Mountains in 1940

Camp Tecumseh

In June of 1945 the train trip from Philadelphia to Meredith was $12.04 and Mr. Grant advised, "Due to wartime shortages of food and manpower, I will ask that each boy be provided with a substantial box luncheon." No transfer of railroad cars to make a direct run around Boston was permitted. On one trip Mr. Gager gave directions at South Station, Boston, to eighty boys who then took the subway to North Station and not one was lost. A few were late but Mr. Gager managed to hold up the Boston-Montreal Express.

Letters to Mr. Grant came from the war fronts. Perot Fiero wrote from England:

December 6, 1943. Dear Mr. Grant: Just a note to tell you how much I missed Camp. When I was on my gun watch . . . I used to sing myself all the hymns of the camp's repertoire. Especially do I remember "Oh Master, Let Me Walk With Thee," also "Brightly Gleams Our Banner," "Lead On Oh King Eternal," and "Now the Day Is Over."

I could get untold enjoyment out of humming the improvisations that Bob Eckles made on the 'Virginia Reel.' I used to sort of daydream of the things that Pete Hires and I used to talk about . . . Remember the time Pinky Shover drove his car down the hill to wash it in the lake, and the brakes never held and the car nearly sunk until the farm horses pulled it out, and when the pump house burned and Whitney ran all the way up to the kitchen to get water . . .

All I can say is "Thanks for the memories" that have given and will always give us rare enjoyment. We will never forget you. Perot.

Perot's father was Pat Fiero who had been at Tecumseh in 1910, and his brother "Beetle" was at camp from 1940 to 1968 and continues his interest. After the war Perot became a priest and suffered an early death in an auto accident.

And from Lt. William C. Scheetz, Jr.:

Aboard the USS Quincy *near Normandy, France. June 18, 1944. [Normandy Invasion was June 6] Dear Mr. Grant: Looking at my Tecumseh Calendar, I find that it is time for another season to start. I just wanted you to know that Bill Sheetz hopes you'll have a successful one. It is one of the things we are fighting for . . . the*

The Chris-Craft returns to port in 1941 with Lew Tabor at the helm.

77

Old timers Jim Gould, David Spooner, Walter Johnson, and
Harry Jones in 1943

Campers dreaming on top of the world, circa 1948

Camp Tecumseh

privilege of a quiet "Tecumseh summer." This comes to you from the shores of France within range of our guns. Old Jerry's waiting for more of the same treatment we handed him on "D" Day when he opened on our ship first of all. . . . This operation will go down as the greatest coordinated effort in history. As father says, we are going to throw another harpoon in Hitler, and then finish him off, and "homeward bound" in a spanking breeze! Sincerely, Bill.

The camp was run on as nearly normal a schedule as possible, even with a shortage of counselors. Mr. Grant had made a good recovery from his above-the-knee amputation of 1939 and still actively directed the program with more delegation to his key council men, including Forrest L. Gager and Alvin S. Wagner who were listed as associate directors in 1944. He deplored giving up all of his active life and insisted on continuing his practice of supervising the noon and evening swim hours. Peter Benoliel in later years had a mental picture of Mr. Grant's perseverance shown by his laboriously climbing (with one artificial leg) the ladder at the end of the pier into the observation booth, and then calling "All in!" No one was permitted in the water prior to this, a tradition of many years.

Mr. Grant's Gentle Discipline

One day after the noon meal, Peter Benoliel was on dish chores. Later that afternoon he received a message from Mr. Grant asking to see him after the Blue-Gray baseball game. Peter went to Mr. Grant's cabin which was near the kitchen door, and Mr. Grant asked if Peter was having a good summer. Of course the answer was enthusiastically in the affirmative. The director then went on to ask whether it was the custom in Peter's family to drink milk from a pitcher. Peter was very embarrassed because he had done just that after the noon meal, and he replied, "No, of course not!" That was the end of the discussion, and Mr. Grant said how pleased he was that Peter was having a good summer. Lessons like this were typical of his gentle but very effective ways of discipline that stuck in the minds of many. Peter Benoliel later became Chairman of the Trustees.

An earlier episode Bill Lingelbach shared was the time he and another counselor decided they wanted to go to town for some evening fun after vespers. It was against the rules for counselors to leave without specific permission. The boys were in bed so the men sneaked out, pushed the old Model T Ford out onto Moultonboro Neck Road so they couldn't be heard, and went to town. Upon returning they pushed the car back where it came from and went to their respective cots to sleep. What a surprise when Bill Lingelbach started to get into bed to find Mr. Grant there. "Where have you been, Billy?" was all that he said. Mr. Grant excused himself politely but the message was very clear to those involved, and the story went all over camp! Behind his back Mr. Grant was sometimes referred to as "The Czar" but in a benevolent way.

Pianist William Kapell, a pupil of Olga Samaroff in Philadelphia, at the age of 20 amazed parents visiting Tecumseh in 1942. He was killed in an airplane crash while on tour just eleven years later.

Farmhand F. Clinton Grace in 1937. A former carpenter, plumber, and builder, his camp pay was $100 per month in 1940.

Farmhand Horace Fife in 1939. He always gummed a half-smoked cigar and when queried about the weather had a stock reply, "Way-ul, it might rain, and then again Gawdammit, it might not. You just caint tell."

Clint Grace's Projects

Farmer Clint Grace died in 1942 at age fifty-two with a legacy of many accomplishments. The perfectly tight and level oak floor in the Lodge still stands as one of his skilled projects. In 1935 he had built the first flush *widow* with the ten toilets. He was also the builder of the walk-in refrigerator in the kitchen which intially had one basic flaw—no handle on the inside of the door. The Red Fox almost turned *blue* one night when he was trapped inside the refrigerator. Bruce Granger was walking near the kitchen on his way to the Senior Campus when he heard a persistent banging noise. Investigating, he found it came from the refrigerator and on opening the door out came Mr. Gager, rescued in time. Another of Clint's major projects was the Intermediate pagoda which was built in 1940. It finally collapsed in 1977 under a tremendous snow load. Clint's wife Ina had predeceased him in a tragic accident in the farmhouse when the pressurized water tank in the cellar under the kitchen exploded and came up through the floor where she was standing. George Hathaway and Horace Fife continued as farmers through this decade.

Pop Stanton Leaves

As the end of the war approached in 1945 another change was taking place with Pop Stanton leaving New Hampshire. He had started as a counselor in 1905 and continued to 1911 when he built a house on Buzzell Cove. From there he came over to camp frequently and kept up his friendship with Mr. Grant.

Phyllis Grant remembered him well. "He had a miserable Boston bulldog, Bimmie, from whom I suffered my first and only dog bite."

Coleridge Edwin Stanton came from Oregon, graduated from Harvard with an M.A. in Greek and Latin which he taught in Detroit for four years followed by twenty years at Pomfret School in Connecticut. Through some stock investments, he made a lot of money. His house burned in 1927 and he was injured. Later he rebuilt on the same ground. The 1941 *Sunbeam* said:

Cole "Pop" Stanton heads out of Buzzell Cove in 1941. One of Grant's oldest friends, he was a counselor first in 1905, and was renowned for his decrepit sneakers, ancient pants, and kleptomaniac habits.

He now has a "snuggery" second to none where his accomplished renditions of Bach . . . float from his magnificent Steinway. But Pop Stanton is most widely known and praised for his culinary accomplishments. All Tecumsites (1905-1911) think back with salivary pleasure on the food he "dished out" on the old-time trips. His six-day menu for the Mt. Washington trip has never been equaled.

He had several idiosyncracies. Phyllis Grant recalled:

He had never married and so his wardrobe was deplorable. He always wore dirty sneakers worn completely through at the toes, pants that should have gone in the rag bag . . . shirts with buttons off and frayed collars, and a once white sailor hat with the brim turned down . . . He was also an occasional kleptomaniac . . .

Once Mr. Grant missed a special china bowl in which he often had his soup in the dining room. So he waited until he knew Stanton had gone to Boston, asked two counselors to go over to

Stanton's cottage and search. They came back with the bowls, towels, and other camp equipment. Then Mr. Grant invited Stanton to lunch and had the waiter serve Stanton his soup in the special bowl. Not a smile from Pop Stanton. The subject was never discussed.

In April of 1946, just before he left for Hollywood, Pop Stanton wrote his last letter to Mr. Grant.

Dear Teacher: I regretted to hear that you have had to cope . . . with illness. We hope your grip on life will be strong enough to carry you through many many years. . . . We sold our camp last October to Dr. Turley . . . and now there will be no more vacationing for us in our cove [Buzzell's Cove]—it is the end of a happy epoch . . . So now for the final chapter—for I shall miss you a whole lot—you and Chandler Post more than any others—May it prove true of all of us, "At eventide there shall be light." We shall think of you often. Yours always, Cole E.S.

(Mr. Grant died six months later.)

A Time For Change

Mr. Grant's Will

In September 1946 Harry (Pushface) Jones and Dave Spooner as "old" alumni came to camp for a visit. As they walked near Mr. Grant's cottage, he called and asked them to come in. He wanted them to take notes on his ideas for the future of Camp Tecumseh and how his will should be modified. On completion they went up to Squam Lake where Bill Lingelbach, Jr. was staying, and the codicil to the will was drafted. The next morning, September 2, 1946, Mr. Grant signed it. Forty-one days later, on October 13, after returning to his Narberth home, Mr. Grant died. At his request, his body was cremated and his ashes spread beneath a favorite oak tree on the knoll on the Hollingsworth Farm near the entrance road.

His will reflected his dedication and unselfishness and his dream for Camp Tecumseh. A portion reads:

Over forty years ago I helped to establish Camp Tecumseh . . . and I have believed in it as a great American institution for the development and training under ideal conditions of a boy's own best self and of his character, qualities of leadership and sportsmanship, and of his ability in various forms of athletic, aesthetic, and manly endeavor. . . . In making the following gift, I devise and bequeath to the Trustees hereinafter named who have had many years of association with the Camp, are deeply interested in its problems, and have shown a broad understanding and judgement in advising their solution . . . I give . . . all my interests in what is known as "Camp Tecumseh" to:

Arthur F. Armstrong, Walter E. Johnson, William E. Lingelbach, Jr., David C. Spooner, Jr., Henderson Supplee, Jr., Lewis P. Tabor, and Henry B. Williams, to be known as "The Trustees of Camp Tecumseh" . . . shall exist perpetually . . . shall not be run for profit but for the purposes aforesaid.

One of his favorite prayers, which he used at vespers at the close of day in the Lodge assembly following a hymn and a brief talk, is appropriate as the Grant era closes:

Oh, Lord: support us all the day long, until the shadows lengthen and the evening comes, and the busy world is hushed, and the fever of life is over, and our work is done. Then in your mercy grant us a safe lodging, and a holy rest, and peace at the last; through Jesus Christ, our Lord. Amen.

Junior C's at Lost River Canyon

Camp Tecumseh

Andy Supplee inscribed this photo to his parents in 1948

Archery with lemonwood bows in the 1940s

Ed Flintermann ready to cross the wake. When water-skis came to Tecumseh after World War II the aquaplane disappeared.

Target practice under Ralph Evans in 1948

A Time For Change

84

Transition to New Leadership

The years from 1946 to 1949 were something of a learning period for the Trustees, and for Al Wagner as he took on full responsibility as a director with the help of Frank Osgood who had come from Penn Charter to coach tennis in 1940. Mr. Grant had wanted Al Wagner to succeed him. Unable to come to breakfast sometimes, Mr. Grant would ask later, "Who sat in my seat this morning?" He was happiest when it was Al Wagner. Porter Shreve (CT 1955–1956) wrote about Wagner,

He grew up playing football on the coal-strewn fields of Lewisburg, Pennsylvania, and he was a rugged competitior. As a coach he used to awaken his sluggish football squad by donning a helmet and scrimmaging with the team. In baseball he had magnificent control as he pitched to them in batting practice, low and inside, impossible to hit. . . . Al got the most from his players. He was always more interested in building character through sports than in winning. . . . Boys liked to come to him because they learned from his wisdom and guidance. . . . At camp I was able to witness the spiritual side of this Christian man, as he often presided over the Sunday worship.

At St. Albans School in 1957 he addressed the students:

A prime requisite of greatness in an athlete is selflessness—a willingness or unconscious desire to put the team above personal glory or gain. . . . Sportsmanship involves being a gentleman at all times in all places.

Because Al Wagner was now at St. Albans School in Washington, he was removed from the principal recruiting area for boys in Philadelphia, and there is some question whether he ever really wanted to be the chief executive officer of the camp, despite his long, valuable, and devoted service to it. Camp Tecumseh has always been strengthened by its share of counselors with long tenure who have kept traditions going through uncertain periods.

Seasoned counselors in the 1948-1949 period, in addition to those mentioned above, included Ralph O. Evans for track and rifle, Tom Fisher for nature, Erwin Drexel for shop and archery, Larry Cloud for gardening, and Freddie James and Tim Hutchinson for milk pasteurizing.

Alvin S. Wagner in 1939. Teacher at Episcopal and St. Albans, Director from 1946 to 1951 and Associate Director until 1962

Camp Tecumseh

Death of the *Thetis*

A minor "tragedy" occurred when the *Thetis* burned about 1943 with Bus Gager witnessing the huge bonfire. Today that relic would have been ideal as a project for restoration of a valuable antique. Likewise the demise of the 1927 Packard took place and the remains were at Bud Whitehouse's garage in Center Harbor where "Beetle" Fiero rescued the Klaxon horn as a memento for his own car.

Jottings

Aurora Borealis

Just before the end of the season in August 1946, Ted Shakespeare (CT 1939-1940, as a boy) recalls ". . . working late in the *Sunbeam* office. When I went outside, I saw the entire sky was illuminated by flickering blue-green, maroon, and icicles of white. It was probably the most spectacular display of Aurora Borealis ever seen in New Hampshire, and I had the joy of waking up the entire Senior Campus to see it."

Jiller

In the early 1930s the Council bought a black and white husky dog named "Jiller" from the Wonalancet Kennels for Mr. Grant. She and her new master became wonderful friends over the years—a very gentle dog, smaller than the huskies that went to the South Pole for Admiral Byrd. Mr. Grant also had a Scottie "Bo-Bo" with quite short legs that used to play and tussle with Jiller. Sadly Jiller died a few months before Mr. Grant's death. He had lost a very close friend at a tough time in his life.

Two Outstanding Cooks

Prior to Mr. Grant's death in 1946 the famous Mrs. Lucy Johnson passed away. How she was able to cook and bake so many tasty foods with wood-

With Larry Cloud at the helm and Bill Gibson perched on the stern, the Thetis *is off on a "carefree" voyage in 1941 powered by her 1925 vintage Star automotive engine.*

burning stoves and bake ovens and without thermostatic controls showed her skills from a different era. Her son-in-law Alfred was dominated by her as he handled kitchen chores, while her daughter Floree did all the laundry each week for 150 persons and hung it all on the line to dry. Lucy Johnson was followed by Percy Stewart, recruited from St. Albans by Al Wagner, whose culinary skills were superb when he wasn't hitting the bottle, a problem that was handled successfully for many years. In spite of, or perhaps because of his problems, Percy was immortalized in an old Tecumseh lament which was often voiced when anything went wrong—"Fizzle, Percy, Thetis."

Pete Benoliel's Good-bye to Mr. Grant

Another recollection of Peter Benoliel's from 1946:

We were having breakfast on the last day before departing for home. Mr. Grant got up at the end of the meal and requested that we all sing "Oh, What A Beautiful Morning" from Rogers and Hammerstein's show Oklahoma. *We did. We then went out and sat on the porch of his cabin. A number of boys stopped by to say good-bye. I was one of them. As I walked up the hill toward the Lodge, I had tears welling up in my eyes, and I had the feeling that I had said good-bye for the last time. It was true.*

7

No Farmer He

1950–1959

WHEN THE TRUSTEES began taking more responsibility for the business affairs and direction of Camp Tecumseh, following Mr. Grant's death, they inherited some obligations to Phyllis and Eleanor Grant and to Forrest Gager which necessitated taking out a mortgage for $27,000, payable by October 13, 1956. A new nonprofit corporation was formed under the name "Camp Tecumseh" and approved by the State of New Hampshire on June 2, 1950. The old Camp Tecumseh corporation was dissolved on November 28, 1950, and the Trustees now had full responsibility to carry out Mr. Grant's dreams for the future.

Before we get into the Munger era, we should look at the camp in 1950 when the waterfront was run by Reds Bagnell (now in the Football Foundation Hall of Fame), Bruce West, and Pete Janetta. Aquaplaning behind the Chris-Craft, named

Tecumseh and driven by Reds Bagnell, was still the only powerboat water sport. Kenny Smith taught sailing with the recently repaired *Comet* No. 1123 (originally made in the Tecumseh wood shop in 1939), and a sneakbox as the only sailboats available. Riding taught by Abbie Belden had been popular with horses Pal, Smokey, Rufus, Honey, and Pee Wee. In an earlier era, the barn had single stalls for seventeen horses which were borrowed for the summer, but interest in riding had now greatly decreased.

This was Bob Glascott's first year at camp at age fifteen. He came up in a station wagon driven by Kenny Smith and on arrival was assigned with Pebble Stone and Fred James to making ice cream and icing the refrigerator. They knew he was new so they put him inside the refrigerator and then proceeded to push in the huge blocks from the icehouse until he was backed way inside, whereupon they turned out the lights and left him for awhile as

---

World Events of the Decade

1950	North Korea invades South Korea.	1955	United States Air Force Academy opens.
1951	Color TV introduced in United States.	1956	Sabin anti-polio vaccine developed.
1952	Eisenhower becomes President.	1957	European Common Market established.
1953	Korean Armistice signed.	1958	NASA established in United States.
1954	Sen. Joseph McCarthy witch-hunts Communists.	1959	Fidel Castro takes over Cuba.

87

an introduction to life at Tecumseh. He still remembers that initiation! In the early 1950s Randy Stone and Dick Pugh (later a Rhodes scholar) made ice cream in a freezer run by a *Woodpecker* one-cylinder gasoline engine that made an infernal racket. You could hear it a long way off and those who knew the operation would run to the back of the kitchen when it stopped and get a big spoon to help clean off the paddle. Mr. Grant gave instructions to keep the amount of flavor to a minimum so no one could be quite sure what flavor it was and thus all would enjoy it. Ice cream making stopped when the cows were sold. The *Woodpecker* died and the pasteurizer was scrapped. Electric refrigeration came in 1953, saddening generations of campers who had toiled in the icehouse and dairy.

Bob Glascott helped farmers George Hathaway and Horace Fife with haying and loading the bales into the loft of the barn. Sometimes those helping could get a ride up to the top on the hay hooks. In the earlier days John Grant, Mr. Grant's nephew, used to work in the hayfield *without* shoes. You are not impressed? Try it sometime.

George Munger Appointed Director

Although Al Wagner and Forrest Gager were running a full camp, Henderson Supplee, Jr.,

Chairman of the Trustees, felt strongly that new ideas were needed. It was at his recommendation, and by his forceful persuasion, that George Almon Munger accepted the job of camp director in 1952.

The timing was perfect to celebrate the 50th Anniversary of Camp Tecumseh and David McMullin III planned a dinner at the Princeton Club on February 29, 1952, "to announce the appointment of George A. Munger as Director of Tecumseh.

Muscle building for football, 1955. George Munger is at the far right, Hunter McMullin's head covers the Trunk Room door, and counselors Jim Gibbons and Sam Niness are in the center and at the right.

No Farmer He

On top of Mt. Chocorua in 1952. Counselors Jim Manley, Ken Clark, and Fred James tower over their charges.

Alvin S. Wagner of St. Albans School, Washington, will continue as Co-Director and Treasurer." The alumni were supportive. The earliest old timers attending included George Orton, 1903, Dave Spooner, 1908, Frank McGill and Eric Finley, 1909, and Howard Ehmke, 1910. A full list appears in the Appendices. They were all invited to a week at camp in September 1952.

Many had known George Munger at the Episcopal Academy when he was captain of the championship football teams of 1927 and 1928; captain of the championship basketball team of 1928-29; member of the championship baseball team of 1926; and set school records in track for pole-vault, high-jump, discus, and javelin. He graduated in 1929 with several awards including the Headmaster's Service Prize.

Others knew him at the University of Pennsylvania Class of 1933 where he played on the varsity track and football teams. After graduating he joined the Episcopal staff as teacher of sacred studies and mathematics as well as football coach where he developed an Interac champion team in 1934, all of whom went on to play college football. Later he returned to the University of Pennsyvania and eventually became varsity football coach from 1939 through 1953 when nine of his fifteen teams were Ivy League Champions, a great record for Penn.

George recalled his start at camp. "Al Wagner didn't seem disappointed when they brought me in and he worked with me as did Pinky Shover. We all got together and made a go of the place." As a man who was used to developing loyal working teams at the University of Pennsylvania, George soon had a team whose ideas he listened to and who immediately set out to improve the facilities and the program. Woozie Supplee said the first year that Munger took over, he had one-hundred applications for counselors' jobs.

The tuition in 1952 was $450 for the eight weeks and this was insufficient to handle the debt problem. It didn't take George long to find out that the dairy operation was losing about $5000 per year. It was nice to have milk and cream for ice cream for two months, but during the rest of the year milk couldn't be sold except in Boston and

88

Equitation at the farm under trainer Abbie Belden

1951 tennis seniors (from left) were John Hubinger, Bill Pope, Dave Hubinger, Randy Stone, Bill Hamilton, Fred James, and Ken Smith. Kneeling in the foreground are Wheeler, Pete Stanley, and an unidentified boy.

No Farmer He

90

The golf putting green under construction in 1952 by Tom Fraser, golf pro and father of Jim Fraser

shipping costs were too high. The cows were sold, haying and planting fodder corn stopped, and then the gardens closed in 1953 except for "Superfood" lettuce which continued until 1956. Dave Spooner after retirement from General Electric reinstituted the corn fields and spent many summers ensuring a good edible corn supply until the camp season was shortened.

A New Emphasis on Sports

With greater emphasis on more sports, George was talking one day in 1952 to Walter Buckley, a Senior (now Chairman of the Trustees), who said, "We need another athletic field." George agreed, so Chester Davis was hired to turn the corn field into Grant Field to be ready for 1953. Since Clint Grace had died in 1942, George Hathaway, the farmer, had moved into the farmhouse with Winnie, his

wife, and about thirty cats. Now Clint's small cottage next to the big barn by the farmhouse was of no use there. It was moved down to the area near the Trunk Room in the woods and became Shover Hall where Bert Shover and his wife Ruth ran the tutoring program.

George Munger brought new life to sports by recruiting some outstanding counselors such as Nelson Yard, Kenny Keuffel, and Howie Dallmar and then introduced *football clinics* in 1952. For the first six weeks of the season boys would be exposed to many different sports and then they could choose a single sport (at first just football) to concentrate on for two full weeks just before camp ended. The boys then returned to school or college ready to be top players in their chosen field. This idea was later expanded to give boys a choice of sports for a real clinic experience and is now a standard part of Tecumseh's program. (This is discussed in greater detail in Chapter 8.)

Camp Tecumseh

Freddy James, Randy Stone, and John Hubinger broadened the choice and range of trips including a Rangeley Lakes canoe trip, a complete traverse of the Presidential Range, a bushwhacking trip to Mt. Shaw through untrodden ways, a two-day Mt. Garfield and Mt. Lafayette trip (with a record climb of 1 hour, 36 minutes, 10 seconds to the top of Mt. Lafayette), and a climb to Mt. Tecumseh for the first time in several years. Four campers proved they could develop a reputation for barefoot mountain climbing: Tex Dampman (Mr. Grant's grandson), Doc Bennett, Freddy James, and Beetle Fiero.

Golf at Tecumseh was primarily an activity for some counselors in the 1920s. With the arrival of Tom Fraser, father of Jim Fraser, a pro golfer from Scotland, the golf program thrived. He reported on the 1952 golf program:

The one thing that George Munger wants is to teach the fundamentals of all sports. . . . I have talked on the origin of golf, the first golf course, and the first golf ball, all of which the Jr. A's and Jr. B's enjoyed. Now that we have almost completed our own golf green, the youth have not only a chance to learn how to play but also how to build a green. . . . When it's all seeded it should be one of the finest short holes in the United States. To Jim Manley, Jack Jackson, Fred James, and Rix Yard . . . a special pat on the back for moving a 500 pound stone . . . and to Bill Lingelbach as the means for getting a junior membership at Bald Peak Colony Club.

For ten dollars each season the boys could have a membership and play there. Tom commented on the course, "Just put a Wee Sprig-o-Scottish Heather at Bald Peak and Tom would be the happiest Scot alive." The Tecumseh green is located by the lakefront to the north end of the beach. By 1954 the grass was well established and in use for practice play.

No Farmer He

The Opera House

In the dramatics area of camp activity, Henry Williams' presence for about two weeks at the end of each season gave the direction that he had begun back in 1921 and in 1931 Henry introduced Gilbert and Sullivan. Then Henry dreamt of having a camp theater building with a good stage, a modern lighting system, and a suitable dressing room attached. He had planted this idea in Mr. Grant's mind when he was a counselor in 1935. From 1947 on Henry kept plugging the project which George Munger finally endorsed in 1955. Former Tecumsite William Cramp Scheetz, Jr. (Henry liked to call him Wilhelm Krampf Schutz), an architect with Savory, Scheetz and Gilmour, drew up the first set of plans on June 24, 1955, for a beautiful building on a slope with permanent seating and fieldstone foundation. There was no money for the estimated cost of $19,975 at that time. Two years later George

Munger was optimistic that more Grant Colony lots (see Jottings at end of Chapter 7) would be sold and in May 1957 suggested Henry go ahead with the theater planning with Lew Tabor and Bill Scheetz so the building would be ready by Tecumseh Day 1957. Lew Tabor with his subtle humor referred to it as "The Williams Memorial Ampitheatre and Hippodrome." The schedule was completely unrealistic for completion in 1957 but the push was on and there was much correspondence back and forth between Henry and Bill Scheetz to come up with a more economical building. Henry was very hard to please as these letters indicate:

November 10, 1957, *Williams to Munger*: "Critical of many details especially with the inclusion of a ladies toilet next to the make-up room of the theatre. Right during the quietest portion of the play the toilet will gush forth with a Wagnerian whoosh as an underlining sound track."

Camp Tecumseh

Cast of the 1950 production of Gilbert and Sullivan "Patience" with directors Walter Johnson and Henry Williams seated in front

November 14, 1957, *Munger to Williams*: "Deeply disappointed the theatre does not meet with your approval. . . . I hope an early heavy snow will maroon you at home so you can devote a few hours to the development of a satisfactory summer theatre for good old Tecumseh."

November 15, 1957, *Scheetz to Williams*: "We are preparing some new sketches which I pray will be the last. . . . About the ladies toilet . . . I have heaved it . . . better not to design this building around a ladies toilet as no matter where it is placed it will be in the wrong spot. . . . Personally I think back of the woodpile or morning glories is the answer."

November 27, 1957, *Williams to Scheetz, Munger and Tabor*, re: latest revisions: "This is fine. I am delighted. Thanks for bearing with me. I love you all. God bless us every one. As ever, Henry."

The Opera House was one of many camp projects in which Lewis Pierson Tabor had a significant part. Lew Tabor was classed as one of the *Fixits* or

Technocrats around camp who lent his MIT training to things mechanical, electrical, and structural. A real photographer with an eye for composition, many of his photographs are included in this history. Lew built a darkroom for camp which has now been converted to the Sunbeam Shack.

As head of the Science Department at the Episcopal Academy, he inspired students to take science seriously and sent a number to engineering careers including Jack Scheetz, Charlie Hargens, and the author. In his evenings his interest in astronomy led him to "put on an old skating cap of a cold winter's night and shoot the stars," as *Time* reported on his work in photographing an atlas of the heavens at the Cooke Observatory near Merion.

Later, after the war, he put his mathematical skills together at the Moore School of Electrical Engineering working on the UNIVAC computer, then to the Franklin Institute as a consultant. As the

No Farmer He

Walter Johnson, lover of the arts and music and part-time leader at Tecumseh, in the 1950s

A production in the new facility in 1960. The curtain was made by Ed Lawless's wife, Sis.

Dr. Frederick James, a true Gilbert and Sullivan fan who acted in Philadelphia, in "HMS Pinafore" during the 1950s

Sunbeam said in 1939, "Quiet, almost to the point of diffidence, he has embarrassed many people by his silences. But in general they are pregnant silences, fraught with productivity!" After long years of being too busy for romance, he married Louise Peterson in 1946 and took her to the home he had built with Bill Scheetz as architect in 1939. Mr. Grant named him as one of the original seven Trustees in his will—a true Tecumseh man with staunch standards. He was a perfectionist in everything he did.

Detailed plans for the *Henry Williams Opera House* were completed, approved by Lew Tabor, constructed by Buster McCormack, and dedicated in 1960. Mrs. Ed Lawless made the new stage curtain. Lloyd Tuttle as music director and counselor participated in the first Gilbert and Sullivan production in the new building before the roof was on.

Although it is now in a field of grass, the site was tree covered and full of rocks to be cleared. Resourceful Buster McCormack with a telephone pole and block and tackle was able to get all the stumps and rocks out by ingenious hard hand work.

Camp Tecumseh

Target practice under the watchful eye of Perot Fiero in 1953

A superb cook, Percy Stewart had the ability to transform any-thing edible into a delicious meal.

Sunbeam *staff circa 1955. From left are: Henry Black, Kecky Jones, David Scott, Hunter McMullin, and Sam Allen.*

No Farmer He

96

Tecumseh Threatened

The future of Camp Tecumseh was seriously threatened in 1955 when proposals for a huge state park came out in the open. One of the sites considered involved taking over all of Camp Tecumseh plus additional adjacent land further out on the Neck totalling 700 acreas at an estimated cost to the state of $557,000. In the off-season Buster McCormack saw some men walking around the Tecumseh property and asked them what they were doing. As soon as he found out the intent to take over the camp, he called George Munger and a suitable defense of Tecumseh's rights was instituted and the property saved.

Staff Housing

For some reason Mr. Grant never favored staff housing by the lake although there was plenty of room for cottages. George Munger had different ideas and with Buster McCormack's skills had a number of buildings moved. Grant's Point Cottage

was inaccessible by road and inconveniently away from the main campus so the decision was made to move it over to the beach to the northwest opposite Joes Island.

Buster McCormack told us how it was done.

It took three years 'cause you gotta have three feet of ice. Starting in the fall . . . I'd go down there and plow the snow off the ice so it would freeze thicker. When it was thick enough, a fellow named Drew from Alton came in, lifted up the house, put big timbers under it and rolled it right down over the ledge, put it on a set of wheels and came right across the ice between the Camp's pier and the islands, right through and onto the beach where it is now.

A woman ran the bulldozer doing the pulling and the ice gave way as they proceeded up the lake, but they never fell through. The cottage had a big fireplace made from stones that Mr. Grant had collected. A local mason, Bob Huston, estimated that tearing it down and rebuilding would cost at least $1500. The mover was so experienced that he picked up the fireplace *with the house* and moved it

without even taking some objects off the mantle. "By God, there was glass things sitting up on the mantel of that thing and they never moved! They never moved from the dusty spot!" Ed Lawless moved into it, then later Terry Cooper, tennis coach from Dartmouth.

Two other cottages from near the Neck Road were moved the next winter and put near the Point Cottage. One is now occupied by Jim Fraser, and the other, formerly Al Wagner's, is now occupied by Bob Glascott.

More About the Sports Program

One of the innovations of the 1950s was the addition of waterskiing for the first time in 1953. The sport had been first demonstrated in France in 1920. In another year a water-ski jump was built and some great jumps made, and some not so great. For safety the use of old football helmets was mandated in case of falls or misses. Then a more conservative era unfolded in a few years when it was decided to abandon the ski jump altogether as too hazardous.

Another sport innovation was fencing when Munger recruited Lajos Csiszar from the University of Pennsylvania as the coach in 1956. This former Olympic coach with a record of excellence became a permanent part of the Tecumseh team for the next thirty-six years. His history is told in Chapter 10. He is known as "Maestro."

With the addition of John Jarvis as soccer coach, another sport was strengthened in the Tecumseh repertoire. John had come over from Scotland in 1949 and was soccer coach at Episcopal Academy. Soccer had special appeal to many boys.

Most of the older traditions of the camp were maintained including the extensive Camp Pemigewasset competitions which had continued with good sportsmanship for fifty years by this period. In one year the Blue-Gray all-season sports events resulted in an amazing exact tie for the all-around medal between two boys, Richie Allman and Pete Stanley. Normally one boy would get a gold medal, second place would receive a silver medal. What to do? George Munger had the two medals cut in two

98

Scraping, caulking, and painting the boats and floats was a regular pre-season chore.

Trainer Bob Glascott instructing in the manly art in the 1950s

Camp Tecumseh

and brazed together, half-silver and half-gold, so that each got the same!

Campers in the 1950s had lots of trip experience as the 1956 Trip Log indicates with a record of 30 trips, 42 trip days, 855 camper trip days, and 124 counselor trip days. George Munger's leadership was off to a great start!

Jottings

The Grant Colony

As a fundraiser Trustees Art Armstrong and Woozie Supplee developed a plan called the *Grant Colony* on Buzzell Cove and continuing around the point along the bay with 200-foot frontage lots laid out for private homes. These were offered to Tecumseh alumni and in a short time Pete Hires, Randy Stone, Bill Hamilton, and Karl Rugart had purchased lots. Using the money raised by the sales, within a few years the mortgage on the camp was paid off, and George now pushed for other camp improvements, some of which were funded through the sale of more lots and some by generous donations from alumni.

Inspections

Cabin and tent inspections were introduced by George Munger with a prize for the best records for the season. In Tom Jarvis' pagoda, Peter Stanley got the idea of spraying some Lysol at appropriate places so when the inspection was made it would at least *smell* clean, and this worked!

Cook-outs

Sunday evenings on the campuses were enlivened by having cook-outs of hot dogs and hamburgers (instead of the former sandwiches) with Percy Stewart continuing the long tradition of cinnamon buns on alternate weeks.

The Store on Moultonborough Neck

Buster McCormack and the store on Moultonboro Neck have a long relationship with Camp Tecumseh. Early in the camp's history it was owned and run by Lynd and Ada Davis. Initially the store was off limits to the campers who were required to purchase all their candy, tin cups, etc. at the camp store. A few of the older boys, however, would occasionally break this rule, living in terror that they would be apprehended by a counselor or even by Mr. Grant. Henry Williams memorialized this perilous journey with a song which ended with the words: "We can not have it, Alex, my boy—impossible."

Mr. Grant was a friend of the Davises and would come up in the spring and stay a few days with them while he opened up his cottage. He used to tell a story about Ada Davis. If you asked her, "Where is your daughter, Ada?, she would say, "She's either in San Francisco or in California, but I don't know which."

Buster McCormack married Doris Davis and took over his grandparents' store in the 1940s. Doris was usually called Dot and was well liked by the boys from camp. Said Buster, "She was a mother. She loved those kids, and those kids would come in. . . . Mrs. Mac, Mrs. Mac. We got along fine. . . . We could trust 'em. We could trust those boys from Tecumseh . . . " This continued into the mid-1970s when the store changed ownership and is now called Jo-Jo's.

8

Thrust for Excellence

1960–1969

DURING his eight years of service at Tecumseh, George Munger had provided more vigorous leadership for the camp than the aging Grant team could offer. This was evident in terms of more successful recruiting, greater emphasis on athletics, a wider range of other activities, and on upgrading of the physical facilities. The Trustees were behind him, the boys loved him, the counselors respected him, and his goals of excellence were clearly stated. All of these accomplishments were reflected statistically as follows: the 1952 roster of 107 campers and 37 staff grew to 157 campers and 44 staff (a ten-year average, 1960-1969). At the same time tuition increased from $450 to $700 but still not enough to cover all needs.

The Clinics

Among Munger's innovations were clinics for more intensive coaching of football and soccer (as mentioned in Chapter 7). The football clinic was started under the direction of Ed Lawless (athletic director and coach at Chestnut Hill Academy in 1961) and involved some sixty campers and counselors. A similar clinic was held for soccer players under Bill Charlton's direction.

Both clinics were open on a volunteer basis to all ages, the purposes being not only to get participants in good physical condition for the coming season, but also to develop skills of punting, passing, blocking, and receiving. This specialized training was instituted without cutting the length of camp season. Although some other camps had split into two sessions with three or four weeks in each, Mr. Munger opposed this idea. He felt that the longer season gave additional time for developing camp spirit and lasting friendships over the years.

Ed Lawless played football at the University of Pennsylvania when Munger was coach there. He

---

World Events of the Decade

1960	First weather satellite launched, Tiros I.	1965	Electrical blackout in northeastern U.S.
1961	John F. Kennedy establishes the Peace Corps.	1966	Edwin E. Aldrin walks in space.
1962	Kennedy vs. Krushchev who withdraws missiles.	1967	World's first human heart transplant.
1963	President John F. Kennedy assassinated.	1968	Martin Luther King assassinated in Memphis.
1964	U.S. attacks North Vietnam bases.	1969	Apollo II makes first moon landing.

served in the U.S. Marines during the Korean War and was director of athletics at Germantown Academy when he first came to Tecumseh about 1955. In 1959 he was head of the waterfront, and later he coached football. He was a key leader on Munger's staff until 1976 when Munger retired. He and Bob Glascott worked together for many years and Ed was married to Bob Glascott's sister.

More Improvements Made

Camp facilities added during the decade included a new wing on the dining hall toward the lake side, a new truck for trips, a fleet of Sailfish sailboats, a Century speedboat for water-skiing, two new cabins for the kitchen staff, two new pagodas, and showers with hot water for the counselors. The kitchen was upgraded with a new floor, an ice-making machine and a new Hobart dishwasher. For improved water supply an infiltration system was installed at the lake so all lake water was filtered through a sand bed before pumping and chlorinating.

Athletic equipment was added to broaden the sports arena for weight lifting and body exercises at the lakefront. A new place was provided for fencing, and for baseball a pitching machine made batting practice fun and available. A major addition was two new tennis courts built in 1968. Badminton and volleyball were also added to the sports game list.

Traveling in the Sixties

Getting to camp in the sixties was a shorter and less challenging trip than the Pullman to New York, boat to Fall River, train to Boston, subway, train, and boat journey of the 1930s, all of which took two days. In 1967 it was reported,

102

Camp Tecumseh opened . . . with the arrival of the camp buses. As usual everyone was perky after the nine-hour ordeal led by Mr. Gager and assisted by counselors Rob Hillas, Bob Freeman, Parson, and Carl "Squat" Henderson. With only one scheduled stop in New York, where the campers loaded up on candy, Coke, and gum, two emergency stops along the way, and a wrong turn in Meredith, the campers arrived in plenty of time for late dinner.

Report on the *Sunbeam*

The *Sunbeam* was published more regularly in the 1960s, but it had suffered after Henry Williams was no longer its inspiration and chief writer. Oddly none of the issues were numbered or dated,

so getting them in order proved arduous. The traditional masthead no longer included the words, "It's the Light That Burns and Not the Heat." It was also hard to know who the editors were because nicknames were the order of the day.

One of the innovations of this period was the inclusion of "SERMONS" in the *Sunbeam*. These were talks given at either the Sunday service for the camp or at the evening vespers held nightly after supper. This was one way of reaching every boy with some of the traditions and goals of the Tecumseh family in line with Christian ideals.

But don't conclude that the *Sunbeam* had lost its sense of humor! It included a page called "TIBBITS" (instead of TIDBITS) with sections like *Seen Around Camp*, most of which are not understandable in today's world. Here are two that do make sense: "Messrs. Gager and Shover reading and

enjoying MAD [Magazine] in the dining room." "Sammy Griffin stealing home."

Quotable Quotes had these: "Please don't damage the Counselors." –Mr. Munger. "Losers never win, you guys!" –Super Sam. "I'm not fat, I'm just short for my width." "Tastiest dinners—Chili Con Carne and Welsh Rarebit."

EXPO '67

Montreal hosted a World's Fair called EXPO in 1967 which George Munger and Beetle Fiero decided would provide an interesting and novel expedition for the seniors and intermediates. Beetle (Erwin A. Fiero, Jr.) as an experienced trip leader was always looking for the unusual. Pat Fiero (Beetle's father) first experienced camp in 1910 and for many years visited camp for a week each year

Under the basket in 1965 are Scott Murphy, Walt Buckley, and Brooks Keffer.

Dan Dougherty supervised construction of the new basketball court.

and slept in the alumni tent at the end of the bathhouse by the beach. Beetle came to camp in 1940 and progressed from camper to counselor, and then to associate director in 1970.

Rainy Days

Rainy days in camp have always created the need for special activities and inside games. Mr. Grant started the custom of postponing the rising time by a half hour on rainy days and this has continued. But 1969 was an exception. This summer was a soaker. The *Sunbeam* carried a special article:

> *With our 2 five-day periods of rain the campers built up an amazing amount of potential energy from their extended periods of sleep.*
>
> *Many new ideas were developed for handling these stores of energy which each camper and counselor had inside him. A group sat on the Lodge porch and listened to the rain pound on the roof while looking out on the soaked Tecumseh fields. One counselor was quoted as saying he was bored silly. We can imagine how 130 boys felt [after 5 days of rain]. Next the Editor of the Sunbeam was seen in his gym shorts sliding down the hill in front of the Lodge on the wet grass which was as slippery as a steep hill packed with snow. Other counselors and campers were soon to follow. Practically the whole camp was sliding down the hill. Our Director and his associates watched the sliding being perfected as boys were going head first on the stomach etc. The world series of Hill Sliding was on August 16. The rain was perfect. It was impossible to see the Lodge from the dining hall. All kinds of records were set . . .*

Doing the Virginia Reel was one of the favorite rainy day activities in earlier days when the number of campers was much lower. With Bob Eckles at the piano this would go on for most of the morning. Stocking feet or bare feet was the custom on the waxed oak floor in the Lodge. The Opera House had not yet been built so activities were limited to the Lodge and Trunk Room. The latter included the Tutoring Room which was a good place to play table games like checkers or chess, or Up-Jenkins (in the 1920s), or even write a letter to a girl friend at Singing Eagle, or as a last resort, a letter to your parents. The craft shop was also an active place in the rain and a time to make a name-plate, sand the bow, make some arrows, or work on a self-directed project.

Another View of Henry Williams

In the drama and music areas, Henry Williams continued to spend at least a portion of his summer devoted to the Gilbert and Sullivan productions. Sam Griffin (at Tecumseh from 1962 at age nine until 1978 as a counselor and now a Trustee) re-membered:

My fondest memories of Camp Tecumseh are centered at the Opera House . . . Henry Williams' direction . . . was the beginning of a love affair with the stage that I have had for the rest of my life . . . Henry could make anyone look good on stage, and he knew just how to teach you to project your voice, move your body, and interact with your fellow actors.

All the while he was rehearsing the show, Henry would also build and paint the sets. He wouldn't be out-side painting and hammering for long before he would have a whole crew of kids watching and doing little bits and pieces for him. If he thought the boy had no talent for building sets, Henry would put him to work pulling weeds around his Opera House.

Henry was quite a character. By the 1960s he had a shock of bright white hair that he wore quite long for that era. He used to say that in his mother's day short hair was the mark of a convict. Henry's costume never varied: button-down white long-sleeve shirt, an old pair of leder-hosen from Austria, white or black anklet socks, and an old pair of moccasins.

He had a wonderful erudite wit and a love of the absurd. He would often talk about the time Mr. Grant laughed so hard at one of the Camp shows that he fell backwards out of the Lodge window. Henry Williams, single handed, kept artistry and culture alive at Tecumseh. He thought it was a good balance after a day of grueling athletics. He was right. I miss him.

Other Griffins including F. Hastings Griffin, Sam's father, and Tyler Griffin, and Tyler Griffin, Jr. also performed under Henry's deft hand and

Swimming races on Tecumseh Day in the 1960s

106

were bitten by the Gilbert and Sullivan bug. All have been active leaders in various Gilbert and Sullivan productions in the Philadelphia area and in the Orpheus Club, a singing group. Terry Griffin (third generation) continued the tradition in 1993.

Henry Williams needed capable pianists to accompany the Gilbert and Sullivan productions with some rather difficult music. In 1961 Curtis York, Director of Music at the Episcopal Academy, was at camp and led many evenings of assembly singing for all. A copy of the first edition of the *Camp Tecumseh Songbook*, dated July 18, 1961, by Curtis York, has survived with twenty–six songs, including "Lord Jeffrey Amherst," "Funiculi, Funicula," "Fight, on Pennsylvania," "Old Man River," and "Walking at Night."

Lloyd Tuttle from the Hill School joined him in 1960 as pianist and music director at Tecumseh and continued for many years up to 1990. He had known Walter Johnson at Westminster Choir College in 1954, and Ralph Johnson at the Hill Camp. He played for the first performance at the

new Opera House in 1960 when the show was produced without a roof on the building.

"Pinky" Shover

Bertram P. Shover, known as "Pinky" around camp, had been recruited by Mr. Grant when Pinky was teaching Middle School at the Episcopal Academy in the 1930s. Then Pinky moved to teach at Grosse Point Country Day School in Michigan. He was small in stature, large in capability as a coach, and a patient and understanding teacher.

Later, in 1977 when celebrating fifty years at Tecumseh, Pinky said:

The summer of 1927 was a great sunshine season and after the first week of camp my chest and belly were so light-red that I was named Pinky and the name followed me through all my years at Tecumseh. His early memory of Tecumseh Day included "The preparing of the famous Tecumseh Punch." Alex Grant and Pop Stanton were the only ones who dared make the punch from their own special recipe. An old iron-stone crockery pot contained the ingredients and the two of them on Saturday morning of

Tecumseh Day, with arms bared to the elbows, used not-long-enough spoons to stir and mix the contents. Many Tecumseh parents and boys did not know they were drinking especially hand- and arm-made beverages on these auspicious Tecumseh camp-closing occasions.

Sam Griffin knew him well as indicated by the following recollection:

Pinky Shover and his wife were the camp tutoring staff. There was never a summer during my years at middle school when I did not spend at least some time in Shover Hall . . . At the time it felt like a prison sentence studying while the other boys played. In looking back, however, I find that some of my fondest memories of Tecumseh revolve around Pinky and the guidance and friendship he offered. Prior to Shover Hall [Clint Grace's old summer cottage] the boys had to study in what is now the junior locker area in the Trunk Room. Pinky used to regale us with stories of trying to tutor boys on rainy days while other campers played ping-pong or were hammering in the shop. It was bedlam. Shover Hall is a quiet and contemplative spot amid the hubbub of daily camp life.

The tutoring program was run like a one-room school-house. Mrs. Shover worked with the youngest boys, teaching spelling, basic grammar, and arithmetic. Pinky worked with the older boys on anything from junior high English to trigonometry. He was amazing. Sometimes the hall would be crowded . . . and Pinky would move from one boy to another, changing subjects and levels with ease. Each boy got the same amount of attention no matter how complicated the subject. That kind of knowledge and discipline are rare in our teachers today.

Pinky also ran the camp store. Store hours were for 20 minutes after lunch and after prayers . . . He had little to sell—batteries, toothbrushes, and stamps. Pinky's Store was actually the camp bank where boys deposited their spending money for the summer. If you wanted money, Pinky would write a check, adjust the balance and have you sign for it. If boys tried to draw out too much money Pinky would lecture them on spending wisely, often questioning a boy on the need for so much spending money.

Pinky also led prayers every evening. He read from the Old Testament and would tell stories about camp and its *founders [following Mr. Grant's tradition]. Sometimes he would read installments from Dr. Balls' book about trips in the White Mountains. It was like an old-fashioned radio serial and he could keep the boys spellbound and quiet for a whole 15 to 20 minutes. He would also run the Sunday services turning to guest speakers from the Senior Staff . . . I think I learned more from those talks about God, Country, manliness and civility than I learned at all my years at school. It was a fabulous education.*

108

As Sam Griffin said:

It was a wonderful time to be at Camp because not only were the Munger years in full swing, but the Senior Staff were people who had worked for and with Mr. Grant in the early years. The feeling of continuity was very reassuring. Tecumseh seemed to be a haven of stability and order during the turbulent decades of the 60s and 70s.

Jottings

Sammy Griffin Day

Sammy Griffin Day was started in 1967 by George Munger when little Sammy, who was "short for his width," asked if there was to be a rest day after Pemi Day when he was exhausted from all the competitions.

To my everlasting horror Mr. Munger stood up in front of the entire dining hall and explained that because little Sammy Griffin was so tired from all the Pemi Day activities, that we would have a Rest Day on the morrow. They arranged it so no bells would ring, no horns would sound, and instead of breakfast, brunch would be served with Percy's homemade donuts.

The Day was forever dubbed "Sammy Griffin Day."

9

Shifting Leadership

1970 – 1979

Munger's Final Years With A Stable Staff

THE STAFF which George Munger had put together in the sixties was functioning well, the major property improvements and much of the needed maintenance completed, and a continuity of the best Tecumseh traditions assured.

In 1970, associate directors included old-timers Beetle Fiero, Ed Flintermann, Jim Fraser, Forrest Gager, Bob Glascott, Ed Lawless, Bert Shover, and Curtis York. Al Molloy, who had come in 1966, and Maestro Csiszar were promoted to associate director status in 1970, and Bruce McCracken in 1974. Beetle Fiero (E.A. Fiero, Jr.), retired after 1970 but remains a Tecumseh man to this day.

What Do You Do For A Royal Prince At Camp?

A boy with famous parents arrived at camp in 1970 at the age of twelve and promptly was nick-named *Albie*. Prince Albert Grimaldi of the Principality of Monaco, and the son of the former Grace Kelly of Philadelphia, was well accepted at camp and soon made friends and participated in camp life. There was some concern for his safety as a royal family son. George Munger recalls having been down at the waterfront

when Bruce McCracken ran down the hill and told me President Nixon would like to speak to me on the phone. I felt it was a joke and told Bruce to tell the President I was swimming and please call back at one o'clock. I had introduced President Nixon as our speaker at a banquet when I was president of the American Football Coaches Association so he knew me. Well, at one o'clock President Nixon did call. He said, "George, I'm afraid of harm coming to Prince Albert while he is in the United States. Will you allow me to send a Secret Agent to Tecumseh?" I agreed and suggested a young athlete would fit into the camp program.

World Events of the Decade

1970	Free market price of gold under $35.		1975	Unemployment hits 9.2%, highest since 1941.
1971	Two new galaxies discovered.		1976	United States Bicentennial.
1972	Dow Jones Index reaches 1000.		1977	Alaska Pipeline opens.
1973	Most wage-price controls end.		1978	Gold rises to $243 per ounce.
1974	President Nixon resigns after Watergate.		1979	Egypt and Israel sign peace treaty.

110

The request was honored with the proviso that the fellow must live and act as a regular counselor. The entire matter was confidential. However, just before the end of camp, the man opened his car trunk when a counselor happened to go by and the radio and other special equipment was visible—his cover had been blown! The idea of such an agent was not repeated in subsequent years when Albie was at camp with Ed Flintermann as his counselor. Above all, Albie wanted to be one of the guys. He didn't want any preferential treatment. In his quiet way he was soon accepted and fit in well.

In 1972 he spent the summer in Europe and wrote to George Munger:

How was Camp this year? Great, I hope! And did we beat Pemi? . . . I've missed camp a great deal this summer, but my gosh, I'll be back next summer. Tom Armstrong (the counselor) just paid me a visit today. He has been cycling through Europe this summer and is going back to school in England very shortly . . . Yours sincerely, Your camper, Albie. GO TECUMSEH.

By 1975 he had earned the right to be a counselor along with Sam Griffin who was quite a prankster, and who went with Albie by canoe up the lake to the home of the camp's music director Lloyd Tuttle one evening and sang Christmas carols out on the lake. Sam later visited Monaco and he and Prince Albert had a great time trying unsuccessfully to evade the bodyguards for a night on the town, even when they tried to escape by climbing out of the window of the men's room at a local restaurant!

An Old and Friendly Rivalry

The 1976 *Sunbeam* expressed it this way:

There's an old tradition, called Camp competition,
That Tecumseh and Pemi have known.
And both have a vision, that the final decision
Will make the hat their own!

Camp Tecumseh

The fiberglass fleet of the Tecumseh navy in 1971

111

The friendly competitions with Camp Pemigewasset continue in what may be one of the longest inter-camp rivalries in New England. *Pemi*, as all Tecumsites call it, was started in 1908 by Dudley B. Reed, Edgar Fauver, and Edwin Fauver and the competitions with Tecumseh began with its first season. With the exception of a few years in World War I, the relationship continues. Thomas Reed, son of the founder and Pemi director when George Munger became director of Tecumseh in 1952, noted that George was wearing a genuine Panama hat. "George, I'd like to have that hat!" George replied, "You can have it if Pemi wins today!"

The custom began and each year the hat went to the winning camp. It became such a symbol that George finally had it metal-plated to preserve it and mounted it on a small pedestal where it is always on display on Pemi Day. Over the years Tecumseh has won it more times than Pemi but the goodwill and sportsmanship between the two camps has continued unimpaired. Meets with Pemi alternated between the two camp locations, Pemi is on Lower Baker Pond near Wentworth, New Hampshire.

A Smooth Transition As A New Director Arrives

The year 1976 was special not only for the United States but also for Camp Tecumseh since it was the last year for George Munger as director after serving twenty-five years. Under his leadership the camp had grown from 107 boys and 37 staff to 192 boys and 52 staff. George was extremely well-liked by boys and staff alike and this posed a tough problem for the Trustees to find a new director since George had decided he wished to retire from full responsibility. He also retired from his position as director and professor of the Department of Physical Education at the University of Pennsylvania, a position he had held since 1952. His first

Shifting Leadership

112

wife, Louise Smith, had died in 1964, and George had plans to marry Viola G. Wieland in 1977. In December 1976 he was inducted into the National Football Hall of Fame as a coach. In 1973 he had been presented with the Distinguished Alumnus Award at the Episcopal Academy. Later he was granted an honorary doctorate by the University of Pennsylvania in 1985.

The Trustees knew that George Munger had become something of a legend and the qualifications for the position broad in scope. The search resulted in the selection of Don McBride to become director for the 1977 Camp Tecumseh season. His background included graduation from St. Joseph's College in 1959, with experience in coaching football and teaching at Malvern Preparatory School for five years, followed by a career at Haverford School where he was assistant football coach, then head basketball coach for seven years. At the time of becoming director of Tecumseh, he had moved into administrative work and was head of the upper school at Haverford. As he said, "I was long on education and kid experience, but very short on camp experience, and none at Camp Tecumseh." After one visit to the site, he took the

Director Donald McBride and three of his five children, Shannon, Don, Jr., and Brian, in 1978. He was director from 1977 to 1983.

Don McBride's wife Joanne with Shannon at the left and Sarah Cooper at the right

Camp Tecumseh

The water-ski jump of the 1970s added thrills, but the spills were hard and football helmets became the fashion for a while. It was finally discontinued because of the hazards.

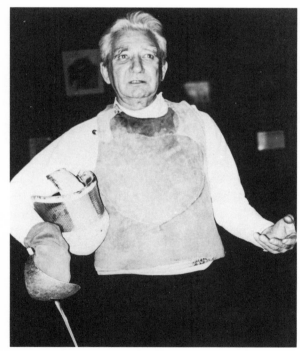

Henry Williams in his native habitat at Dartmouth in 1978

Maestro Lajos S. Csiszar in 1975, an inspiring Olympic fencing coach from Penn who has taught at Tecumseh from 1950 through the present.

Shifting Leadership

114

The infirmary in 1970. Two rooms were added at the rear in 1974.

job in November 1976. With enthusiasm and a smooth transition helped by George Munger, a high percentage of returning campers, and a loyal staff, the year 1977 was excellent with total boys and staff membering 239 versus 244 for 1976.

Don and his wife Joanne and their five children came up in June of 1977 and moved into the farmhouse which at that time was the director's residence and office. The Trustees soon had a new cottage built at the lakefront just below the Junior pagoda (The Rock) for George Munger to use during summers and still be available to give Don McBride an on-site consultant to help in understanding the Tecumseh traditions.

Young hurdlers demonstrate their techniques in 1975.

Shifting Leadership

Heavy snows suring the winter of 1975 brought down the venerable lodge porch.

In 1977 extraordinary snow demolished the intermediate pagoda as well and resulted in the decision to move its site some 300 yards south of the main waterfront.

In the summer of 1977 a new intermediate pagoda took shape and was dedicated to Pinky Shover as "Pinky's Pad." The twin of this pagoda built nearby in honor of George Munger was named "House of George."

As always the camp buildings needed repairs. George Munger thought that perhaps the Lodge with its poor foundation beams should be replaced with a modern building but was soon vociferously talked out of that idea by Henry Williams. (It became known in 1993 that part of the Lodge was built in 1778). Henry pointed to many traditions and memories about the Lodge including the huge number of names painted on the walls and ceiling as a significant historical record. George Munger sent out a special appeal and funds were donated to restore the building without losing the interior. Randy Stone succeeded Forrest Gager as treasurer in 1972 and the Lodge restoration was the first of many property renovations he organized. Randy retired in 1986 with many improvements completed and the financial condition in sound shape.

Art Armstrong as president of the Trustees had a plan developed for the 130 acres behind the Grant Colony on Buzzell Cove. It was proposed to have canals dredged, a clubhouse erected, and a significant number of lots with lake access for boats included. Referred to as "Armstrong Acres," the idea never was implemented. The policy was accepted to sell an occasional existing lot as capital funds were needed beyond what could be raised from alumni solicitations.

Don McBride took a walk around camp in April 1979 and discovered that the Intermediate pagoda had been completely demolished by the heavy snow load. With only three months to opening, Bob Peaslee and Sons took on the job and two buildings were erected on a new site about 300 yards south of the dock and bathhouse. These were named *Pinky's Pad* and *House of George* in honor of Pinky Shover and George Munger, and a new road was added to them in this undeveloped part of the camp.

The water supply from the lake was being examined and for long-term safety a drilled well was attempted and stopped at 500 feet as a dry well. The infiltration system was still giving good water quality, and further drilling was therefore postponed until 1993 when an excellent deep well was completed.

Camp Tecumseh

Boys Giving Something Back —Founder's Week

In 1978 Jim Fraser, associate director for many years, came up with the idea of *Founder's Week* following Mr. Grant's philosophy that "the greatest attribute is a sense of service." During this week each group of campers and their counselors give freely of their time to improvement projects around the camp such as painting buildings, clearing brush in the woods, hauling off old lumber from repair projects to a burning place, and improving borders of roads or playing fields. Each year the week has been named for an old-timer. First it was Mr. Grant, then Dr. McCracken, then Doc Orton, followed by Pinky Shover, Forrest Gager, and Al Wagner. Others included Percy Stewart, the great cook for many years, and Buster McCormack as long-time maintenance man, all persons who gave of themselves for a better Tecumseh. Peter Benoliel was so honored in 1992. He had been chairman of the Trustees for a time. As Jim Fraser explained, "The fun part of it is the Rookies, the Junior 3s and Junior 2s who are never allowed to paint at home, and they just have a ball!"

Jottings

More Sunbeam *Gems From the "Tibbits" Pages of the '70s*

Bobby Glascott – "If I freeze to death on Mt. Washington, my father will kill me!"

Ed Dailey – "It's raining today so we can't ski since there will be puddles on the lake."

Mike Jannetta (while swimming to Bald Peak, a two-mile swim) – "I want to swim from Camp to Bald Peak because from Bald Peak to Camp is uphill."

The Legend of Mary B – Truth or Fable?

Mary B (for Bewalader—?) was an inmate of the old Moultonboro Poor Farm who became insane and was confined to one of the cells in the basement of what is now the Lodge. As her condition continued to worsen, in a fit of melancholia she gathered up her chains, escaped to the main floor, and proceeded to hang herself from one of the Lodge rafters.

You don't believe it? Well, Jim Fraser runs orientation tours for the Rookies (first year boys), and he shows them the remnants of the basement cell and points out the actual rafter she used and her grave on Camp property. If they aren't too frightened by all that, he will then go on to explain that every summer on her birthday night—August 13—her ghost reappears and roams about camp perpetrating untold atrocities. Sometimes a canoe appears on the Lodge roof. One year Mr. Gager's car was found on the float. Another time the dining tables were all set up on the lawn for breakfast.

Beware on August 13th!

10

Continuity In The Ninth Decade

1980 – 1992

Pressures of the Eighties

DON MCBRIDE was having second thoughts about his ability to cope with the time demands of being Director of Camp Tecumseh and at the same time do his job at Haverford School with equal quality. Recruitment of boys for camp was getting to be a major time consideration and had to be done when school demands were heaviest. Nevertheless the Trustees were behind him and encouraged him to stay on. The quality of the program was there, and both Don and his wife Joie were well-liked and respected. Enrollment started to drop and went from 190 boys in 1979 to 172 in 1980.

The Camp Store

Many boys had gotten into the habit of eating too much candy and junk foods which Don McBride felt was undesirable. Therefore, he tried to curtail the trips to the store across the road from camp which was now owned by Russ Beznoska under the name Jo-Jo's.

He also discouraged "care packages" from home since he wished to emphasize a balanced diet free from extra sweets. Boys now came with more funds in their pockets and resented the restriction to such a degree that it was finally rescinded. In 1980 the *Sunbeam* said" "We're wondering when guards will be posted to prevent intermediates from going to Jo-Jo's." Later an ice cream stand was set up at the farm where boys could buy ice cream at specified hours as an alternative to store visits. Unfortunately Jo-Jo's also sells beer and a few boys would try to buy it surreptitiously.

World Events of the Decade

1980	Mt. St. Helens blows top!	1987	INF Treaty signed by Gorbachev and Reagan.
1981	Reagan becomes President.	1988	Surgeon General makes recommendations.
1982	ATT broken up in anti-trust suit.	1989	Berlin Wall falls.
1983	Supreme Court upholds Roe vs. Wade.	1990	Germany reunited. Iraq overruns Kuwait.
1984	Vietnam Memorial dedicated.	1991	50th Anniversary of Pearl Harbor.
1986	Challenger Space Shuttle explodes.	1992	Bill Clinton elected President.

118

Tecumseh Behavior Standards

Historically the Tecumseh tradition had always been that "Tecumseh boys don't drink." George Munger had spelled this out clearly in a letter to all counselors in 1974 as follows:

Traditionally counselors at Tecumseh do not smoke or drink. Exceptions have been made allowing smoking, however, we count on your good judgement, and believe smoking should be inconspicuous, certainly never smoke while coaching. . . . Obviously, alcohol is taboo at camp. Be sure you never bring so much as a can of beer on campus. When off duty for lunch or dinner, even with parents, please no cocktails if you must return to camp for regular counselor duties. No counselor can achieve respectful leadership if a camper knows you have had a drink.

Equally clear was the policy on use of drugs— "even experimenting with 'pot' or drugs will subject a camper to immediate expulsion."

Drinking among the high-school-age group during the 1980s had become an increasing problem which Tecumseh could not tolerate. One parent wrote, after reading some of Tecumseh's principles, "I must say, if Tecumseh is a bit old-fashioned and conservative, so am I and I am most pleased to have a son privileged to be exposed to its precepts."

Sports Emphasis

In the early years the major emphasis was on baseball, football, tennis, and water sports like rowing, canoe races, and swimming. Now the most popular sports were tennis, soccer, and lacrosse. Swimming, sailing, and water-skiing had increased in popularity but aquaplaning was a thing of the past. Basketball was growing under Dan Dougherty.

One sport with a unique history at Tecumseh was fencing under the direction of Maestro Lajos Csiszar, who, as previously noted, first came to Tecumseh in 1956 when he was the U.S. Olympic Coach that year. Interestingly he was born in 1903 when Tecumseh was founded, and he continues at Tecumseh through its and his 90th year. "Maestro," as he is known around Camp, was Hungarian-born and trained. At the University of Budapest, he

attained "national all-star" status in fencing and soccer. After graduation in 1932 he soon was recognized as one of Europe's foremost fencing coaches and in 1936 was coach of Hungary's Olympic fencing team. He led the United States team in the World Championships of 1970. Coaching at the University of Pennsylvania, his fencers were on every United States fencing team for more than twenty years starting in 1952.

Attesting to Maestro's physical condition, he won a Tecumseh tee-shirt in the newly established obstacle course in 1980 for the fifty and over class.

Impeccable technique under the watchful eye of Maestro Csiszar in 1993

On The Tecumseh Stage

The Gilbert and Sullivan tradition continued with Mark Luff becoming director in 1979 following the skilled leadership of Hastings Griffin and his son Sam, each having been trained by Henry Williams. With Lloyd Tuttle and Dave Shaw at the pianos, Henry Williams continued to come down from Dartmouth for some back-up before opening night. After the production of the Mikado in 1980, it was announced that the Opera House, started in 1959, "which finally realized Mr. William's fondest hopes, will henceforth be known as the *Henry B. Williams Opera House*. His first production in the

1930s was *Trial By Jury*. . . . His interest, time, and effort in each production year after year cannot be measured." He died November 26, 1987, at eighty years of age as Professor Emeritus at Dartmouth College, and as one of the original Trustees of Camp Tecumseh named in Mr. Grant's will.

Mark Luff goes over the score with "Pinafore girl" John Tuck.

More Mountains To Explore

When Don McBride asked Jay Luff to head the trip crew, lots of new adventures resulted. Jay had come to camp in 1962 at age twelve and continued through most years since. He attended Episcopal Academy, then finally was graduated from Germantown Academy.

Jay likes to race up mountains, and he can handle groups of twenty-five or thirty boys with suitable counselors to bring up the rear. With radios at the front and rear of the line, all can be kept together safely. The seniors have some challenging trips such as the Mt. Katahdin three-day-trip to Baxter State Park in Maine. They establish a base camp with tents for shelter unlike the old days when only ponchos were available for overnights. The intermediates do the Presidentials sometimes with overnights at the Appalachian Mountain Club Lakes-of-the-Clouds and Madison huts without need for camping gear.

Jay introduced another first at Tecumseh with trips to Mt. Marcy in the Adirondacks, about four-and-a-half hours away by van. The use of open trucks with benches for transporting boys on mountain trips was prohibited in the eighties and now a van or bus is used for the boys and a pick-up truck for the gear.

Jay worked closely with Ted Handy, another mountain climber who had twenty-five years' experience at a girls' camp prior to starting at Tecumseh in 1976. He was a teacher at Germantown Academy. A true nature lover, he is an unusually well-informed teacher with forty years of fantastic experience on dozens of trails in the White Mountains. In recent years he has enjoyed taking the smaller boys on less rugged mountains and less travelled trails along streams. For the younger boys Red Hill (renamed Mt. Rouge by Beetle Fiero to make it sound bigger), Mt. Major, Mt. Rattlesnake, Mt. Percival, Mt. Morgan, and Mt. Welch are typical hiking destinations.

Camp Tecumseh

George Munger, inspiring leader of men and boys, in 1982

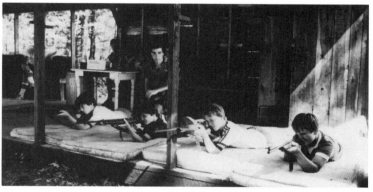

Marksmanship in 1982

1988 NRA award list and Pro Marksman patch

Counselor Mark Luff with children at the special post-season week in 1985 for children with cancer.

A Change In Leadership

In 1983, his seventh year as director, due to continuing time conflicts with his Haverford School job, Don McBride resigned and urged the Trustees to find a full-time director for 1984. Enrollment was down to 121 boys in 1983 versus 189 in 1977. Jay Crawford who was now Chairman of the Trustees replacing Art Armstrong, who had served from 1970 to 1979, formed a special search committee to find a new director. Jay was Headmaster of the Episcopal Academy and a former counselor.

Among the candidates was Richard Roe who had retired early from the business world and was now teaching at Haverford Friends School on a part-time basis, and travelling with his family in Europe during summers conducting soccer tours for boys. Richard, forty-two years old, was a great sports enthusiast in squash, golf, tennis, volleyball, and walking. (Since then he won a U.S. National Championship in Doubles Squash in the age 50 category in 1993.) At the University of Maryland he was co-captain of the soccer team which in 1962 was number two in the United States with

Camp Tecumseh

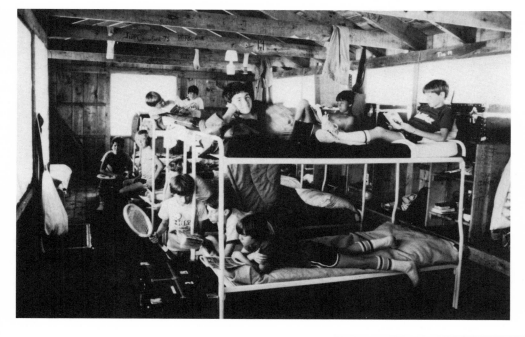

Richard as the top scorer with twenty-seven goals. He was married to Margaret Ann (Meg) Davis, and two of their boys, Richard, Jr. and Chris, had been campers at Tecumseh in 1977.

Starting in April 1978, the family took off on a round-the-world visit to twenty-nine countries ending in Australia where Richard wanted to live. Because Rich and Chris missed Camp Tecumseh so greatly, they returned in time for the 1979 season. Then in 1980 Gabby also became a camper.

Richard, with some knowledge of how much the camp meant to his boys, decided to make this his next career choice. He had worked with investment and brokerage firms F. I. DuPont, W. E. Hutton, and Kidder Peabody from which he had retired in 1978. Trustees Walter Buckley and Gerry McGinley had known him in the business world a few years earlier.

Richard Goes To Work, Camp Thrives

Richard Frederick Roe prefers to be called Richard. His first effort was to boost the enrollment through hard work, with less than a year to

Fletcher (Terry) Cooper, Tecumseh director of tennis since 1977, shares in the special camp for young cancer patients in 1985.

124

the start of the 1984 season. By the time camp opened in June 1984 there were 212 campers and a staff of 60, an increase of 103 total campers and staff! In his first year as director, all nine seasoned associate directors returned except Pinky Shover who had retired. Richard added eleven more counselors and changed the title from associate directors to senior staff. Four were new including John Smith, Frans Borghuis, and Gary Marsman from the Netherlands, and Ted Handy who returned after a year's absence. It was a great transition team to continue the Tecumseh traditions and to help guide a new director in summer camp operation.

The continuing need for capital funds and scholarship aid was partly met by Jay Crawford's establishment of a Blue-Gray Fund supported by loyal alumni and friends. Richard pushed for more tuition aid. Said he, "I had attended a camp in New Hampshire as a youth on a scholarship. I wanted other boys with limited financial resources to have

such opportunities." Aided in part by a robust economy, Blue-Gray Fund giving quadrupled, so that by 1993 thirty-five boys were able to come to Tecumseh supported in part by this fund.

Continuing the overall camp facility improvement objective of the Munger/McBride era the ten years of the 1980s witnessed some very substantial property improvements including enlarging the dining hall, renovation of the eight tennis courts to professional standards, major electrical equipment for the Henry Williams Opera House, a new and larger widow (toilet facility), a new director's cottage, new Senior tent platforms, farm equipment, two ski boats, a bus, a weight-lifting center, and a recreational building for the counselors. By the end of the ninth decade the camp property was in excellent condition.

One of Richard's early additions to the camp program was the CIT (Counselors-in-Training) activity for boys showing promise as future counselors. At the end of his first season in 1984 the

Dan Dougherty gives the boys some fine points.

125

Sunbeam dedicated the final issue to "The Director and His Wife." Meg had helped in many ways also.

Increased interest in basketball stimulated by Dan Dougherty, coach and math teacher at the Episcopal Academy, led to the addition of a second paved basketball court and lighting for evening use to extend the hours of informal play. Dan's ability to develop basketball skills was lauded by many boys. Dan first started at camp in 1977.

The eighties saw the continued development of the football clinics as Jim Fraser shared his professional skills as coach and athletic director. One *Sunbeam* added an extra page "In Appreciation of Jim Fraser Whose Hard Work Was A Great Inspiration." Jim's seven years in professional football with the Broncos, Kansas City, and the New England Patriots ending in 1967, had given him the impetus to make him a great coach at Tecumseh as well as at the Episcopal High School in Alexandria, Virginia. He started at Tecumseh in 1948 as an Intermediate under Randy Stone.

Jim Fraser shows the way in a punting drill

Continuity In The Ninth Decade

126

Will Kain slides into second as Ted Swain goes for the tag.

Water Activities

Tecumseh water activities lent special emphasis to training in sailing, canoe handling, and swimming skills under the direction of Mark Luff as new waterfront director in 1984. The Tecumseh fleet comprised 3 ski boats, 10 Sunfish sailboats, 2 Laser sailboats, 7 sailboards, 12 canoes, a float, and a ski jump. Bill Colman taught waterskiing. Three extended canoe trips included a 5-day camping and 75-mile canoe trip near Jackman, Maine, led by John Schneider and Ric Roe, Jr. on the Moose River where the seniors "spent our first dinner watching a moose feed on the weeds across the river. It wasn't too big, only about 9 feet tall—to the shoulders!" The intermediates covered part of the Androscoggin River in northern New Hampshire. "To say the least the trip was exciting and awesome. Fast water and rapids made the trip exciting and wet, and Eric Carlson and Dave McMullin received the Captain Nemo Submarine

John Armstrong shows Brandon Abney how it's done

The new float built in 1979 and shown here in 1982 was remarkably similar to the 1905 configuration.

Vic Di Nubile and Mike Padula in the two-man shell

The thrill of the slalom ski in 1993

Continuity In The Ninth Decade

Unmarked natural stones in the graveyard of the Moultonborough Poor Farm (1849-1890), photographed in 1992

Award for taking in the least water, but flipping the most." Juniors paddled thirty miles on the Saco River in Maine where it is a flatwater river good for beginners.

With four new Mishal sailboards and a windsurfing simulator, Keith Moore taught every camper basic techniques of windsurfing without even getting wet. Five campers went on to race in the Meredith Bay speed trials.

The swimming goals of having every boy learn the four basic strokes, set by Bob "Z Man" Zullinger (and assisted by Andy Baxter and Ian Anderson) were nearly reached. "It was a fantastic year on the water."

Terry Cooper presided over a broad-based tennis program where the eight courts were always busy, and the results showed in outside competition. Said Terry, "Our strongest level of competition was in the fifteen-year-old division and in the twelve and under. We swept Pemi, won the Alton Bay tournament, in addition to blanking Belknap, a truly outstanding record for the twelve and unders." A new feature added in 1984 was a tennis ladder in which 125 boys participated at all age levels. In 1986 with major financial support of Trustees Don Graham and Peter Benoliel the eight tennis courts were resurfaced with four inches of clay, and top-dressed with slate dust to make truly professional courts. Tournaments at Tecumseh were started in 1989 with Alton, Birchmont, Pemi, Winaukee, Robinhood, and Samoset participating. With 60 to 70 percent of Tecumseh boys returning each year and with a seven-week season including two final weeks

Camp Tecumseh

of concentrated clinic instruction, Tecumseh players became tough competition.

Safety has always had high priority in all camp programs since the camp was founded in 1903. Recently John and Ellie Smith, as athletic trainer and nurse respectively, have been an active and caring couple in accident prevention and treatment. John first attended camp in 1976.

Work Teams That Make Tecumseh

The work ethic so essential for a smooth running camp continued in the eighth decade as part of the Tecumseh family traditions. One of the important crews is the KCAC, the Kitchen Crew Athletic Association. Under the direction of Bob Glascott, about sixteen campers and others are involved in all functions of feeding the camp except cooking and baking. They set tables, wait on tables, and run the dishwashing machine and keep the dining hall neat and clean. Some are part-timers. Some get scholarship help. It is always fun to be close to the cooks where food favors are possible. The 1992 final *Sunbeam* was dedicated to Mr. Glascott who not only was responsible for feeding over 200 persons at each meal but also took care of the physical plant and its crises.

Another great work group is the four- to six-man tennis crew which has the never-ending job of keeping the courts brushed and rolled. Missing from the early morning tennis chores were the visits from Mr. Grant who used to come to the courts before breakfast, bringing everyone his favorite health food, a glass of orange juice and a raw egg that they would drink!

The farm and maintenance superintendent was now Peter W. Beede who had taken the place of the McCormacks in 1980. He had his own herd of seven cows but the campers had no part in their care unlike the "old days." Peter and his father built the Munger Cottage.

In season a small maintenance crew, directed by Bob Glascott and Ed Flintermann as "Mr. Fixit," does a lot of the odd jobs and repairs around camp.

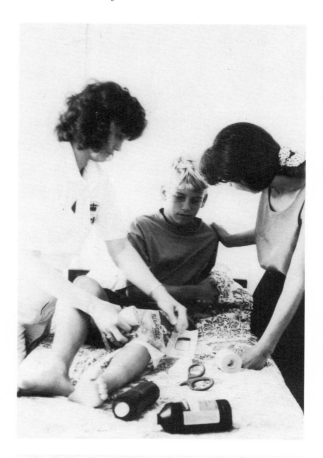

129

Thanks for the memories. In 1991 the Shackers were Dan Ward, Brett Miller, Pete Gillin, and Honorary Larry Cofsky.

130

Keeping Interested Friends Informed

Jay Crawford as Chairman of the Trustees in 1978 started an *Alumni Sunbeam* to bring news about the camp to the loyal interested alumni. The message of the 1981 issue was, "Some things never change." Jay Crawford spelled out the continuing philosophy of the camp which in part said,

An enjoyable summer experience has been assured by a life released from over-organization and regimentation. . . . The staff encourages self-discipline while exercising just and kind supervision over the campers, supporting the notion that superior leadership inspires fine living—service to each other and to the camp. The boy who benefits from a season at Tecumseh is one who is eager to find an atmosphere of freedom where effort toward improvement is encouraged and where mental, moral, and physical growth are concurrent.

Richard Roe picked up on this idea and wrote a regular letter to "The Friends of Camp Tecumseh" starting in the fall of 1984 and continuing twice a year. It was his idea in 1984 to start collecting memorabilia, photos, and items from the past to be stored in an archives room in the farmhouse, the existence of which was invaluable in making this book possible. His first letter said:

Camp Tecumseh has always been, and will remain, steeped in tradition. . . . A 1925 camper returning for his first visit in fifty-nine years was stunned to see how little had changed. . . . The farmhouse and barn, Lodge, Trunk Room, Dining Hall, waterfront, are much as they were then. And yes, all of the plaques and names are still up in the Lodge.

The Tournament Era Begins

Although Tecumseh has always had competitions with other camps, it has been with one camp at a time. In 1988 Mark Luff started a new trend with a soccer tournament at Tecumseh in which Winaukee, Pemi, Kingswood, and Belknap participated at various age levels. Terry Cooper followed in 1989 with the Tennis Tournaments, then Jim Gibbons, who had been recruited by Don McBride from Bishop McDevitt High School, arranged the "First Tecumseh Invitational Track 'Meet'" in 1989. These continued and in 1992 the scores for one meet showed Tecumseh 603, Pemi 343, Marist 93, and Winaukee 92. Thus this became not only an exhibition for Tecumseh talent but a good time is had by all.

Something For Every Boy In The Eighties

Opportunities for every interest and skill level continued to be developed. For free time there was a horseshoe court, a new sand bed volleyball court at the beach, a weight-lifting area near the dock, a rope climb on a big pine by the beach, a tetherball court, two new paved basketball courts next to the Trunk Room, and the baseball pitching machine which Don McBride had added.

An Iron Man Competition was started which included a swim to the island and back (later changed to a swim to the women's beach near Glascott's cottage), followed by a 2.1 mile run. Typical times ranged from 20 minutes 45 seconds up to 44 minutes 47 seconds for the smaller boys. The mini-marathon became popular with a 4.2

Erik Strid pumps iron while Chris Roe checks the technique in a new weight lifting building near the bath house.

mile running course over the camp's dirt roads and trails. In many of these activities awards were made in every age group from the nine-year-olds to the twenty-six and older category. Top Gun was the fierce volleyball competition game with two players on a side.

Fishing has always attracted loyal adherents. In 1989 the Pinky Shover Fishing Award competition had 45 campers participating with 93 fish caught and one dog! Samire Poles caught Jay Luff's dog Onyx who was watching at the beach. "She was writhing around with two hooks in her nose, gasping for air. Samire tried to submit Onyx as his entry in the fish contest in the category of 'Dog Fish' but was disqualified!" The winner was Drew Guzy, son of the camp nurse, Shelly. His four-pound bass caught on his birthday won the prize.

At Season's End

Starting in 1903 an annual Tecumseh Day has always been held, an event which many parents

Camp Tecumseh

attend when awards and medals are given to the boys who have excelled in camp activities over the summer. The "Tecumseh Boy Awards" are announced to recognize one boy at each of the senior, intermediate, and junior age levels who have shown the attributes of manliness, service, loyalty, and leadership, and represent the best in Tecumseh ideals. Many of these boys continue their Tecumseh journey as junior counselors, and eventually become counselors. A listing of the recipients of the Tecumseh Boy Awards appears in the appendices as well as listings of some of the named awards for other activities.

Farewell To The Ninetieth Year

At the end of a recent season a camper wrote in the *Sunbeam* these timeless words for campers and alumni:

While sitting in a dreary classroom this winter, you may find yourself dreaming of a place many say cannot be. You'll look back on the people you loved and the times you treasured! Remembering the operetta, the showers that felt so good after sliding on the wrestling mat, TECUMSEH. Not just a memory, but a real place . . . Best of all it's filled with new and more exciting thrills every summer. So be good to yourself and your fellow man . . .

133

Epilogue

ONE DICTIONARY defines epilogue as "a concluding section that rounds out the design of a literary work." Since no one, least of all this author, would pretend to call this collection of historical data and memorabilia a literary work, the heading is perhaps inappropriate. Nevertheless, a brief summation may be in order.

What is there about Camp Tecumseh that has inspired such affection and loyalty in the hearts and minds of the hundreds of boys and men who have spent summers there? After all, it is only seven or eight weeks of the fifty-two which make up the year, and thus relatively insignificant compared to the eight months spent annually for sixteen years in school and college. And yet for a great many the experience of those few weeks leaves as deep an im-

print on their lives as do those other institutions.

The best answer to the above question can probably be found in the way in which the camp has successfully met the challenge inherent in the following statement made by Alexander Grant in 1937:

"Tecumseh came into being to supply a certain human need to the growing boy; to emancipate him from the intense regimentation of our city and school life; to regulate his sense of values which so often become twisted or lost. In such an environment as we have here, with lakes, mountains, and forests about us, where things of beauty live and grow, the soul and body of the boy would grow in harmony with his surroundings."

If the past be prologue, Tecumseh will surely live another ninety years!

Sunrise, 1993

134

Appendices

Directors and Trustees

DIRECTORS

Honors and Awards

The earliest photographs of Camp Tecumseh show a variety of silver cups that were awarded for excellence in various camp activities. Since then a wide variety of awards have evolved. The Tecumseh medals in bronze, silver, and gold with a head of Chief Tecumseh as the motif, have been given at the end of the season for every sport, and for various age levels from Seniors to Junior III (formerly Junior C). Some special awards have been established in honor of specific individuals whose service to Tecumseh is thus perpetuated.

THE SENIOR TECUMSEH BOY

Established in 1927 this award is given to the Senior Boy who by vote of the Senior Campers typifies the spirit of Camp Tecumseh with emphasis on manliness, service, loyalty, and leadership. A plaque donated by Ernest Scott (father of David R. who was Tecumseh Boy in 1954) with the names of all previous Tecumseh Boys is awarded and held by the winner for one year. Starting in 1989 the Senior Tecumseh Boy also received a $2000 scholarship to an instituiion of higher learning from the $35,000 bequest of Arthur F. Armstrong who was a counselor at Tecumseh in the 1920s and later Chairman of the Trustees from 1970 to 1979. Mr. Armstrong continued his enthusiasm for Tecumseh until his death on September 29, 1987. His ashes were spread at the camp at his request.

1928	Emory Eysmans	1931	William F. Tiernan, Jr.	1934	Drew I. Pearsall
1929	Philip W. Townsend	1932	Edward Lane Stanley	1935	Robert McDonald
1930	Hayes Aikens	1933	William Richards	1936	Benjamin Lee Bird

Camp Tecumseh

1937	George N. Degerberg, Jr.	1956	Matthew W. Black, Jr.	1976	Hugh McC. Coxe
1938	Edward Charles McDonald	1957	Donald Metz	1977	James C. McCracken
1939	George E. Stanley	1958	David W. Wilson	1978	Robert X. Allman
1940	Andrew G. Knox	1959	G. Spencer Garrett	1979	Joseph P. McGrath
1941	John R. Roberts, Jr.	1960	Frank Craig Heston	1980	Morty Fertel
1942	William J. Ryan	1961	Edwards A. Fleming	1981	William W. Keffer
1943	Theodore Coxe	1962	William A. Warnock III	1982	Timothy C. O'Shea
1944	---	1963	Johnson Poe Duer	1983	Robert L. Gray IV
1945	Richard Pugh	1964	Louis A. Young, Jr.	1984	Matt Oelkers
1946	John M. Hume &	1965	McKinley "Sandy" McAdoo	1985	Matthew Micolucci
	Richard Ryan	1966	---	1986	Ted Durkin
1947	Frederick S. Allen	1967	Ben Russell	1987	Howie Goodwin
1948	Erwin A. Fiero, Jr.	1968	Graham F. Zug	1988	Songha Willis
1949	William Pugh, Jr.	1969	Scott Tyson Davis	1989	Pancho Mazza
1950	Timothy Hutchinson	1970	Steven C. Ramsey	1990	Don McDonough
1951	---	1971	Keith W. Forster	1991	Mike Reardon
1952	Scott Murphy	1972	Allen E. Stiner, Jr.	1992	Mike O'Shea
1953	William G. Hamilton III	1973	Thomas J. Edwards	1993	Doug Ormond
1954	David R. Scott	1974	Peter C. Abronski		
1955	Porter G. Shreve	1975	John McGinley & Peter Monaghan		

137

THE ALVIN S. WAGNER INTERMEDIATE TECUMSEH BOY

Starting in 1983 this award was established to recognize those boys of Intermediate age (boys who have finished 8th Grade) who in the opin- ion of their fellow campers meet the criteria like the Senior Tecumseh Boy qualifications. Al Wagner was at Camp Tecumseh from 1928 to 1962 and director from 1947 to 1951. He headed the Senior Campus for many years.

1983	Matthew D. Oelkers	1987	Andy Gribbel	1991	Mackey Pierce
1984	Ted Durkin	1988	Brandon Wyszynski	1992	Luke Tickner &
1985	Howie Goodwin	1989	Dan McFadden		Geoff Watson
1986	Brian Murphy	1990	Ryan Tickner	1993	Will Hiesinger

THE JUNIOR TECUMSEH BOY

Beginning in 1936 the Kenneth H. Bitting Trophy was given in the form of a large bowl inscribed with the winners. This was awarded annually to the Tecumseh boy of the Junior Divisions who in the opinion of his fellows was most outstanding for his courtesy, his manli- ness, and his service to the camp. At the time it was established it was awarded to any boy below Senior age which included Intermediates. Since 1983, with the beginning of the Alvin S. Wagner Intermediate Award, only boys below Intermediate age were eligible and the method of election modified. Each Junior cabin nomi- nates one boy, and the entire Council then makes the final selection from those nominated. Kenneth H. Bitting donated the trophy because of his early experience at Tecumseh in 1915 and his desire to foster Tecumseh ideals. He served with distinction in both World War I and World War II and died in 1970. His son Kenneth H. Bitting, Jr. of St. Louis, was there in 1936 and played Lady Ella in *Patience* at age twelve.

1936	Louis Robert Knodel	1957	William Jessup	1976	James L. Crawford III &
1937	Lawrence Pugh Cloud	1958	Robert A. Haines		John T. Gillin, Jr.
1938	Andrew Randolph Stone	1959	David R. Strawbridge	1977	Vincent L. Allman
1939	Joseph Donald Goodman	1960	Edmund Lukens Harvey, Jr.	1978	Kurt Colehower
1940	Clinton Newbold Ely	1961	Johnson Poe Duer	1979	Kenneth Burns &
1941	Henderson Supplee III	1962	Rodman A. St. Clair, Jr.		Jonathan T. Colehower
1942	Warren Tutt Stone	1963	McKinley C. McAdoo	1980	Timothy C. O'Shea
1943	Frederick Stetson Allen	1964	Bruce McCracken	1981	Timothy C. O'Shea
1944	Nathaniel Richard Bowditch	1965	Jeffrey S. Young	1982	John L. Lawton
1945	Erwin Agnew Fiero, Jr.	1966	Lee K. Andrews	1983	Stephen Skillman
1946	Scott Swain Withrow	1967	Scott T. Davis	1984	Stephen Skillman
1947	William Osgood	1968	Rodman W. Smith	1985	Don Mann
1948	Michael M. Stewart	1969	John L. Spofford	1986	Marc Tousignant
1949	Jack Pinheiro	1970	Drew E. Spaeth &	1987	Geoff Walker
1950	William G. Hamilton III		David L. Walker	1988	Geoff Watson
1951	Farish Jenkins	1971	Stephen G. Yarnall	1989	Mike O'Shea
1952	Winthrop B. James	1972	B. E. Clay Spurgeon	1990	Jamie Griffin
1953	William S. Flippin	1973	John McGinley	1991	Geoff Watson
1954	Peter Gehret	1974	P. Adam Abronski	1992	Will Kain &
1955	Franklin B. Smith	1975	James C. McCracken		Matt Schuh
1956	Allan E. Walker III			1993	Will Hiesinger

Appendices

THE PETER BENOLIEL TENNIS AWARD

An award for "good sportsmanship, faithfulness in service and dedication to the game of tennis" was the way it was described in 1980. More recently "to the camper showing consistent interest, sportsmanship, and improvement in tennis." Peter Benoliel was a counselor from 1948 to 1951 and tennis coach at Tecumseh while he was at Princeton in 1950-1951 and became Chairman of the Trustees from 1985 to 1990.

THE FRANKLIN OSGOOD MEMORIAL TENNIS AWARD

The best tennis player in the Junior Camp received this award for several years. Frank Osgood coached tennis at Tecumseh from 1941 to 1948. Frank Osgood, Jr. also coached in 1948.

THE WILLIAM E. LINGELBACH SOCCER TROPHY

"For skill, dedication, and heart on the soccer field," this award is presented to the outstanding player of the year at Tecumseh. Bill Lingelbach, Jr. was a camper in the early 1920s. He was named to the All-American Soccer team while a player at the University of Pennsylvania, and while in England as a Rhodes Scholar was invited to join the American Olympic Team. The trophy is one of his soccer shoes bronzed and mounted. He is one of the Trustees appointed in Mr. Grant's will in 1946.

THE JOSIAH C. MCCRACKEN FOOTBALL TROPHY

This trophy was first awarded in 1974 "to the boy who has shown promise towards developing those qualities of leadership, loyalty, effort, spirit, and skills in the game of football." It is a mounted silver football given by James S. Collins, Jr. in memory of Josiah C. McCracken, one of the founders of Camp Tecumseh, and who had been named to the All-American football team while at the University of Pennsylvania in 1899.

THE WALLACE GREENE ARNOLD TRIP AWARD

Started in 1979 this award is presented "for constant interest and appreciation for Tecumseh's trip program" which included mountain climbing, camping, and canoe trips. It was proposed by alumni of the Toltecs, the camp which Wallace Arnold founded in the 1930s. He was a counselor at Tecumseh in the 1912 era, and a close friend of Mr. Grant for many years.

THE JOHN A. GLASCOTT TRACK AND FIELD AWARD

Named for the father of Robert Glascott, John H. Glascott was a track coach at the University of Pennsylvania and a counselor at Tecumseh from 1961 to 1965. The award was established in 1967 and annually given "for excellence in track and field."

THE MAESTRO L.S. CSISZAR CHAMPIONS TROPHY

Started in 1956 this award goes to the best boy in fencing at Tecumseh. Maestro Csiszar has coached fencing at Tecumseh since 1956 and continued through 1993 at age 90, an age record for the counselor staff. Unequalled, he was winner of the Founders Week Award twice in 1983 and again in 1993!

THE ALEXANDER GRANT AWARD

Established by the Trustees in 1993, this award is "Presented by the Trustees to a former camper or staff member who has distinguished himself and Camp Tecumseh through his service to the Camp and to his community at large."
The first award was made to George A. Munger on May 6, 1993, at the 90th Anniversary Reunion held at the Episcopal Academy, Merion, Pennsylvania, and presented by Walter W. Buckley, Jr., Chairman of the Trustees of Camp Tecumseh.

Camp Roster, 1910

The earliest complete list of campers and staff is that for 1910 and is given here based on the dining room seating list arranged by tables.

1. Dr. Orton	2. Mr. Grant	3. Mr. Snyder	4. Mr. Edson
Bell	Johnson, W.	Rebmann	Adair, S.
Davis	Kennedy, A.	Schaum, F.	Beard
Elliott	McCormick, L.	Smeltzer	Brown
Fetterolf	Mahan	Smyth	Delany
Finletter	McGill	Tily, Harry	Duer
Fritz, G.	McKinley	Spooner	Ehret, S.
Gray	Norris	Tily, Herbert	Finley
Haddock	Poulterer	Townsend	Fisher
Mr. Shryock	Mr. Lewis	Herr Meyer	Mr. Van Pelt

5. Dr. Spaeth	6. Mr. Lester Ehmke	7. Mr. F.H. Ehmke	8. Mr. Wharton
Gould, J.	Schaum, C.	Adair, I.	Flagg
Grubb	Riley	Allen	Fritz, C.
Kelly	Sloane	Blagden	Genung

Camp Tecumseh

5. Kennedy, K.
    McCormick, G.
    Murdock, L.
    Platt
    Prettyman
    Mr. Frazier

6. Sparks
    Stout
    Sweeney
    Weston
    Whiting
    Mr. MacKenzie

7. Clapp
    Ehret, R.
    English, E.
    Evans
    Fiero
    Mr. Hansl

8. Grandin, E.
    Gundaker, C.
    Howell
    Johnson, E.
    Kennedy, D.
    Mr. Stouffer

9. Dr. Bixby
    English, G.
    Gould, S.
    Granding, F.
    Gundaker, G.
    Haynes
    Keser
    Klien
    Lathrop

10. Mr. Stanton
    Koons
    Mason
    McCall, S.
    Murdock, T.

11. Mr. Bannard
    Hariss
    Whelan
    Zimmermann
    Vogt
    Whiteside

Camp Roster, 1976

DIRECTOR

Munger, George A., Villanova, Pennsylvania

ASSOCIATE DIRECTORS

Csiszar, Louis S., Lansdowne, Pennsylvania
Flintermann, Edward, Malvern, Pennsylvania
Fraser, James, Champaign, Illinois

Gager, Forrest L., Newtown Square, Pennsylvania
Glascott, Robert A., Norristown, Pennsylvania
Lawless, Edward B., Dresher, Pennsylvania

McCracken, Bruce, Littletown, Massachusetts
Molloy, Albert G., Jr., Wayne, Pennsylvania
Shover, Bertram, Grosse Pointe Park, Michigan

TREASURER

Stone, Randolph, Newtown Square, Pennsylvania

STAFF

Glascott, Mrs. Robert A., Norristown, Pennsylvania
McCormack, Leroy (Buster), Camp Tecumseh, Center Harbor, New Hampshire

McCormack, Howard, Camp Tecumseh, Center Harbor, New Hampshire
Spooner, David C., Jr., Wayne, Pennsylvania
Curry, Albert, Summit Point, West Virginia

Lark, Elliott, Philadelphia, Pennsylvania
Lomack, James, Temple, Pennsylvania
Stewart, Percy, Washington, D.C.

COUNSELORS

Abronski, Peter C., Miami, Florida
Armstrong, John, West Vancouver, B.C., Canada
Cooper, Garey, Merion, Pennsylvania
Donaldson, Barton H., Wallingford, Pennsylvania
Fetting, Mark, Baltimore, Maryland
Foster, Jon, Needham, Massachusetts
Fritz, David, Media, Pennsylvania
Gilbert, David H., Allentown, Pennsylvania
Handy, Edward H., Jr., Philadelphia, Pennsylvania
Harkins, J. Graham III, Devon, Pennsylvania

Kain, Stephen R., Haddonfield, New Jersey
Kaminski, Joseph, Danbury, Connecticut
Kempf, Florian, Philadelphia, Pennsylvania
Luff, Mark C., Wayne, Pennsylvania
Luff, Paul B., Wayne, Pennsylvania
Luff, Jay, Wayne, Pennsylvania
Francois-Poncet, Andre, Paris, France
Lyons, Chris, Newtown Square, Pennsylvania
McGinley, John, Short Hills, New Jersey
Molloy, Michael S., Wayne, Pennsylvania
Neal, Hunter S., Jr., Bryn Mawr, Pennsylvania

Quiggle, James, Washington, D.C.
Quiggle, Thomas E., Washington, D.C.
Riley, Madison, Newtown Square, Pennsylvania
Shaw, David, Willow Grove, Pennsylvania
Smith, John, Philadelphia, Pennsylvania
Smith, Lewis duP., Paoli, Pennsylvania
Stone, Bruce, Haverford, Pennsylvania
Sturla, Donald, Jr., Villanova, Pennsylvania
Taylor, Robert G., Wallingford, Pennsylvania
Tuttle, Lloyd, Pottstown, Pennsylvania
Walker, David L., Center Harbor, New Hampshire

SENIORS

Abronski, Adam, Miami, Florida
Baldwin, Charles, Weston, Massachusetts
Brandt, Jefferson D., Wayne, Pennsylvania
Brucker, Bradford, Grosse Pointe Farms, Michigan
Burdick, David O., Wayne, Pennsylvania
Carpi, Colin, Princeton, New Jersey
Carpi, David, Princeton, New Jersey
Castle, Joseph L., Jr., Gladwyne, Pennsylvania
Chadwick, Charles B., Jr., Bryn Mawr, Pennsylvania
Clark, Ladd, Southborough, Massachusetts
Coxe, Hugh McC., Gladwyne, Pennsylvania
Cummin, G. Jeremy, Jr., Wayne, Pennsylvania
Flood, Robert M., Fort Washington, Pennsylvania

Fritz, Andrew, Wayne, Pennsylvania
Fuqua, Gerard A., Cornwall-on-Hudson, New York
Groves, Charles P., Berwyn, Pennsylvania
Harper, Bill, Fort Lauderdale, Florida
Heaver, Philip A., Jr., Newtown Square, Pennsylvania
Jackson, Mac R., Paoli, Pennsylvania
Latta, Thomas W., Devon, Pennsylvania
Mattis, Bruce, Wayne, Pennsylvania
McAlaine, Robert D., Wynnewood, Pennsylvania
McConnell, Michael J., Devon, Pennsylvania
McCracken, James C., Plymouth Meeting, Pennsylvania

Meister, Carl J. III, West Chester, Pennsylvania
Neff, Bill, Devon, Pennsylvania
Northrup, Philip W., Haverford, Pennsylvania
Osgood, Stephen M., West Nyack, New York
O'Shea, Daniel, Garden City, New York
Poff, James A., Jr., Philadelphia, Pennsylvania
Rugart, Eric S., Haverford, Pennsylvania
Simmons, Cheston, Jr., Malvern, Pennsylvania
Smith, Henry B. duP., Paoili, Pennsylvania
Szabo, Tom, New York, New York
Tornetta, Lawrence F., Jr., Norristown, Pennsylvania
Trimpi, Richard, Allentown, Pennsylvania
Wilder, Gordon H., Penn Valley, Pennsylvania

Appendices

INTERMEDIATES

Allman, Robert, Philadelphia, Pennsylvania
Anastasi, Lawrence J., Swarthmore, Pennsylvania
Arnold, Thomas W., Gwynedd Valley, Pennsylvania
Berkowitz, Henry, Jr., Villanova, Pennsylvania
Bradbeer, James B., Jr., Philadelphia, Pennsylvania
Camp, William E., Haverford, Pennsylvania
Connor, Robert W., Jr., Philadelphia, Pennsylvania
Cosslett, Christopher E., Rosemont, Pennsylvania
Crawford, James L. III, Merion, Pennsylvania
Dailey, Edward G., Lemoyne, Pennsylvania

DiEugenio, David, Lionville, Pennsylvania
Fitzgerald, William A. III, Haverford, Pennsylvania
Fleming, David W., Jr., Princeton, New Jersey
Fuqua, Joseph B., Cornwall-on-Hudson, New York
Gaston, Herbert P., Haverford, Pennsylvania
Gerber, Thomas, Swarthmore, Pennsylvania
Gillin, John T., Jr. Wyndmoor, Pennsylvania
Gillin, Robert M., Jr., Bryn Mawr, Pennsylvania
Glascott, Robert A., Jr., Norristown, Pennsylvania
Gordon, Irv, Gladwyne, Pennsylvania
Harrity, Thomas W., Rosemont, Pennsylvania
Levy, Robert P., Jr., Bryn Mawr, Pennsylvania

Maschal, John Bell, Swarthmore, Pennsylvania
McCloskey, John, Malvern, Pennsylvania
McDevitt, Malvern, Pennsylvania
McGinley, Gerald O., Short Hills, Pennsylvania
Molloy, John A., Wayne, Pennsylvania
Myers, David, Ardmore, Pennsylvania
Pailas, Dean C., Ambler, Pennsylvania
Peter, Marc E., Gilsum, New Hampshire
Rieger, Richard D., Grand Rapids, Michigan
Ryan, Richard, Jr., Devon, Pennsylvania
Sharp, Bob, Valley Forge, Pennsylvania
Tornetta, Paul A., Norristown, Pennsylvania
Wearner, Christopher R., Evergreen, Colorado
Witlin, John J., Gwynedd Valley, Pennsylvania
Zullinger, Robert L. III, Gladwyne, Pennsylvania

CROW'S NEST

Allman, Vincent, Philadelphia, Pennsylvania
Busson, Arpad A., Beaulieu, France
Colehower, William H., Philadelphia, Pennsylvania
Colehower, Kurt, Los Altos Hills, California
Cook, Clyde W., New Milford, Pennsylvania
Coxe, Theodore S., Jr., Gladwyne, Pennsylvania
Crawford, Stephen, Merion, Pennsylvania

DeLaura, Michael L., Bryn Mawr, Pennsylvania
Jannetta, Peter T., Pittsburgh, Pennsylvania
LeBien, Laurent C., Larchmont, New York
Manwaring, John L., Jr., Ottsville, Pennsylvania
Manwaring, Roy A. II, Fort Washington, Pennsylvania
McGrath, Joseph P., Jr., Short Hills, New Jersey

Palmer, Edgar S., Jr., Merion Station, Pennsylvania
Peebles, David S., Crawfordsville, Indiana
Peter, Michael S., Gilsum, New Hampshire
Shields, J. Todd, Gladwyne, Pennsylvania
Tornetta, Stephen A., Norristown, Pennsylvania
Yeomans, Andrew W., Berwyn, Pennsylvania

LOOK OUT

Bell, Robert K. III, Ocean City, New Jersey
Cassatt, Alexander J. III, Wayne, Pennsylvania
Castle, David, Rydal, Pennsylvania
Doyle, Steven J., Nashua, New Hampshire
Edwards, Neill, Radnor, Pennsylvania

McCloskey, Robert, Malvern, Pennsylvania
McCormack, Michael, Center Harbor, New Hampshire
Nichols, Mark, Andover, Massachusetts
Ogren, Jeffrey W., Villanova, Pennsylvania

Payne, David Whitney, Sarasota, Florida
Sharp, Brian, Valley Forge, Pennsylvania
Shatz, Geoffrey I., Bryn Mawr, Pennsylvania
Shoemaker, Peter, Chatham, New Jersey
Thompson, Barry, Sarasota, Florida

THE SHIP

Allman, Richard J., Philadelphia, Pennsylvania
Baur, Hart, Miami, Florida
Cashman, John A., Wilmington, Delaware
Compton, Eric B., Swarthmore, Pennsylvania
Cullen, Woody, Devon, Pennsylvania
Dailey, John R., Lemoyne, Pennsylvania
Dailey, Mark A., Amherst, New Hampshire

Edwards, John E., Clayton, Missouri
McAlaine, Michael B., Penn Valley, Pennsylvania
McKaig, Kevin B., Bethesda, Maryland
McMullin, H. Brooke, Haverford, Pennsylvania
Murdoch, Carter, Rosemont, Pennsylvania
Osgood, Donald W., West Nyack, New York
Phillips, Blaine T., Jr., Wilmington, Delaware

Reohr, William R., Wallingford, Pennsylvania
Ryan, James W., Devon, Pennsylvania
Van Schaick, David L., Jr., Newtown Square, Pennsylvania
Walsh, Larry, Haverford, Pennsylvania
White, Chester, Villanova, Pennsylvania

MACK'S SHACK

Albin, Alejandro, Bosques de las Lomas, Mexico
Beardwood, Jr., Fort Washington, Pennsylvania
Chrystie, James, Short Hills, New Jersey
Duffy, John C., Short Hills, New Jersey
Gordon, Richard, Gladwyne, Pennsylvania
Greber, Kevin, Merion, Pennsylvania

Hauptfuhrer, Bruce A., Gladwyne, Pennsylvania
Jones, Richard I. G., Jr., Coatesville, Pennsylvania
Kelley, Scott, Huntingdon Valley, Pennsylvania
Martineau, John, Gladwyne, Pennsylvania
McGinley, Mark H., Short Hills, New Jersey
Samson, Bruce L., Blue Bell, Pennsylvania

Saul, Larry, Short Hills, New Jersey
Splendido, Joseph A., Jr., Lafayette Hill, Pennsylvania
Ward, Nicholas S., Short Hills, New Jersey
Ward, Rodman III, Centerville, Delaware
Whittlesey, Henry C., Haverford, Pennsylvania

ALUMNI

Angelus, Ted L., Westport, Connecticut
Cappetta, Jon Michael, Concord, Massachusetts
Cook, R. Wallace, New Milford, Pennsylvania
Cresci, Michael P. E., Vineland, New Jersey
Cruz, Ricardo, Olivar de las Padres, Mexico
Dooner, Keith, Linwood, New Jersey

Fertel, Morty, Springfield, Pennsylvania
Francois-Poncet, Alexis, Paris, France
French, Arthur E. III, Short Hills, New Jersey
Garrett, Arthur S., McLean, Virginia
Gilmore, Charles P., Longport, New Jersey
Havens, David A., Gladwyne, Pennsylvania

Moore, John C., Willoughby Hills, Ohio
O'Brien, Gavin W., Presque Isle, Maine
Peter Gregory, Wayne, Pennsylvania
Riefsnyder, Howard, Devon, Pennsylvania
Whipple, John, Cherry Hill, New Jersey
Yeomans, Paul H. III, Devon, Pennsylvania

140

Camp Tecumseh

NEW PAGODA

Allman, Lee, Philadelphia, Pennsylvania
Bermudez, Carlos, Santiago, Dominican Republic
Cassatt, Anthony D. II, Wayne, Pennsylvania
Crockett, Frederick G., Gladwyne, Pennsylvania
DiEugenio, Scott, Lionville, Pennsylvania
Drake, Craiger, Philadelphia, Pennsylvania
Draper, Benjamin H. B., Concord, North Carolina

Glascott, Scott J., Doylestown, Pennsylvania
Hache, Simon, Santo Domingo, Dominican Republic
Jannetta, Michael, Pittsburgh, Pennsylvania
Keffer, William W., Wayne, Pennsylvania
LeBien, Thomas E., Larchmont, New York
Lewis, Ross P., Philadelphia, Pennsylvania

Maschal, Peter, Swarthmore, Pennsylvania
McGrath, Brian T., Short Hills, New Jersey
Nichols, Scott, Andover, Massachusetts
Odell, Stuart, I., Jr., Gladwyne, Pennsylvania
Peuffier, Robert A., Wellington Road, London, England
Ryan, Robert M., Jr. Gwynedd Valley, Pennsylvania

THE ROCK

Baur, Craig, Miami, Florida
Buford, Anthony A. III, Gladwyne, Pennsylvania
Butcher, McBee, Jr., Bryn Mawr, Pennsylvania
Cassatt, Jacques G., Wayne, Pennsylvania

Chandlee, Blakeley, Jr., Rosemont, Pennsylvania
Fitts, Alan C., Rosemont, Pennsylvania
Fraser, John, Champaign, Illinois
Geisel, Stuart, Haverford, Pennsylvania

McMullin, Scott P., Rosemont, Pennsylvania
O'Shea, Timothy, Garden City, New York
Walsh, Billy, Haverford, Pennsylvania
Walsh, Emon, Haverford, Pennsylvania

50th Reunion Attendees, 1952

NAME	YEARS AT CAMP	NAME	YEARS AT CAMP	NAME	YEARS AT CAMP
Shover, B.P.	27, 31-52	Fiero, Beetle	40-46, 48-52	Johnson, Ralph C.	15-16, 26-40
Lingelbach, Wm. A., Jr.	19-26, 29, 30	Orton, George W.	02-24	Arnold, Wallace Greene	12-17, 19
Williams, Henry B.	21, 22, 23, 25-38	Carnwath, Joseph W.	26, 29-34	James, Fred	40-44, 46, 47, 49-52
Johnson, Walter E.	14, 15, 16, 17, 19, 20, 21	Gay, H. Burton, Jr.	20	McMullin, David 3rd	20-29
Stanley, George C.	29-42, 46	Griffin, F. H., Jr.	38-42	Hamilton, William G., Jr.	21-27
Stanley, Robert G.	36-42	Evans, Ralph O.	39-51	Pearsall, Drew	24-39
Munger, Herbert N., Jr.	27	Tiernan, W. F., Jr.	28-38	Griffin, J. Tyler	37-41
Harman, William H., Jr.	23-25, 28-31	Aikens, H., Hays, Jr.	24-33	Mayer, Harry C.	36, 40, 41
Yocum, J.G. Gordon	31-40	Pakradooni, Aram P.	31-39	Schwartz, Matheson C.	14, 15, 17, 20
Ehmke, Howard	10, 11, 12	McGill, Frank	09-13	Gager, Forrest L.	24-52
Munger, George A.	52	Finley, Eric B.	09-11	Arnold, Nathan P.	17, 18
Supplee, Henderson, Jr.	17-25	Card, William E.	20-23, 44	Steinmetz, Philip Hausser	20
Ortlepp, William H.	25, 26, 28	Smith, E. Newbold	38-42	Wagner, Alvin S.	25-52
Fiero, Pat	10	Putnam, Richard C.	34-41, 46	Spooner, David C., Jr.	08-16 plus many, many more.
Fiero, E. Perot	34-41	Stone, Randolph	38-42, 44, 46-52		
		Chase, Arthur C.	25-29		

Founders Week Dedications

Early years	Alexander Grant	1981	George A. Munger	1988	Randy Stone
	Dr. Josiah McCracken and	1982	Alvin S. Wagner	1989	Buster McCormack
	Dr. George Orton	1983	"Maestro" Csiszar	1990	Bill Lingelbach
1979	"Pinky" Shover	1984	Forrest L. Gager	1991	John H. Edwards
1980	Percy A. Stewart	1985	Edward Flintermann	1992	Peter Benoliel
		1986	Arthur Armstrong, Jr.	1993	"Maestro" Csiszar
		1987	Henry B. Williams		

Information Sources

University of Pennsylvania Archives. Files on Mike Murphy, George Munger, and L.J. Csiszar with photographs.
University Liggett School, Grosse Pointe Woods, MI. Joan Dodenhoff, Archivist for Bertram Shover information.
Illustrated History of St. Albans by Porter Shreve. Tributes to Alvin S. Wagner.
"As I Remember Moultonborough." Frances Stevens, Harvest Press, 1988.

Cemetery Records of Moultonborough, New Hampshire edited by Rev. Frank E. Greene, 1988. Moultonborough Historical Society.
Central and Northern Title Co., Inc. Kenneth Lovett for help in early deed searches.
Dartmouth College Archives – Henry Williams material.
The Story of the Olympic Games. John Kiernan and Arthur Daley.

Appendices

Illustrations

143

Index

144

Index

Camp Tecumseh

has been published in a first edition
of twelve hundred and fifty copies.
Designed by A. L. Morris,
the text was composed in Bem
and printed by Knowlton & McLeary
in Farmington, Maine on Cougar Opaque Text.
The jacket was printed on Warren's Lustro Offset Enamel Gloss,
and the endleaves on Curtis Tweedweave Text.
The binding in Holliston Mills' Roxite
was executed by New Hampshire Bindery
in Concord, New Hampshire.